BOOK MARKETING
is dead

Book marketing secrets you MUST
know BEFORE you publish your book

A CREATIVINDIE GUIDE BY
DEREK MURPHY

Thanks for purchasing this book!
You can share any of the tips in here, but please refer or link.
If you need help with anything, feel free to get in touch.
A short review on Amazon would be hugely appreciated.

Sincerely, Derek Murphy

Twitter: @creativindie | Facebook.com/creativindie

Sincere thanks to Donna Joy Usher, author of the *Chanel Series*, for helping weed out a bunch of typos from this book.

creativINDIE

TABLE OF CONTENTS

GREETINGS 7

WHAT THIS BOOK IS ABOUT 11

HOW THIS BOOK IS ORGANIZED 16

WHO I AM 17

STAGE ONE 19

THE BASICS

Creating Your Author Platform 30

STAGE TWO 75

BUILDING SOCIAL KARMA

STAGE THREE 107

MARKETING

CONCLUSION 153

ABOUT THE AUTHOR 159

If you've bought this book I'm assuming you have or will soon have a book out on the market, and are exploring ways to turn it into a best-selling powerhouse that will slaughter the competition and pay for your retirement. The indie publishing world is thrilling because of the possible returns, and I hope you and your book do well.

You're probably searching for things like "book marketing" and "book promotion" so you can learn how to find readers and convince them to buy your book.

But almost everything you read will be wrong.

That's because marketing in general is dead. Advertising is dead. Selling and convincing people to buy—also dead. The new law of booksales is this: if you're talking about your book, promoting your book, sharing your book—you're screwing it all up.

I had a 30-second Twitter conversation recently with Jonathan Gunson (founder of Bestseller Labs and Creator of the "Twitter for Authors" course) that went like this:

"Authors who constantly 'shout' their books
on Twitter and Facebook, and do NOTHING
ELSE will soon find themselves ignored."

I mentioned all the author marketing books I've been blazing through, looking for actionable tips and resources for this book—many of which are still giving advice that is "Old School."

Old fashioned book marketers and promoters will say you need to hustle, you need to push, you need to keep getting out there day after day to tweet, like, share, chat and do SEO and lots of other complicated stuff. Recently I've also been noticing a lot of bestselling authors put out short little ebooks about how THEY sold a ton of books but are light on practical advice.

Most of them sold a lot of books through sheer force of will and constant soap-boxing and pestering everybody they know... but reached their sales goals (and then wrote a book about book marketing!) Unfortunately, while this kind of marketing *can* work— these authors were successful *despite* some very big flaws in their platform and their marketing campaigns, and it's hard for them to see what actually worked and what was holding them back.

In self-publishing circles, thought-leaders on book marketing are often tragically inexperienced authors who managed to sell a lot of copies, and hence became "experts"—even if their methods aren't that great. And their tactics are still being copied although marketing has drastically changed (even just in the last year!) When I look on my Twitter or Facebook feeds, I see ninety-nine authors doing it wrong, and only a few doing it right, which means the advice out there for indie authors isn't good enough.

One reason is that indie authors still have a huge chip on their shoulder. Although self-publishing is becoming more and more acceptable, there's still doubt and skepticism. If you tell someone you published a book, they might raise one eyebrow and ask, "Did you *really* publish it, or did you just *self-publish*?" This makes indie authors feel like tiny voices screaming against a dark cruel world, trying to get the word out and give their book a chance.

Don't start off assuming everyone is against you. But you also shouldn't think and act small. Don't just be the loudest voice in the room. Don't just tell people how great your book is. Find a way to connect, to be the story. Marketing has actually become very easy—you build trust and you get people to like you.

"Stop presenting and start connecting."

That's the new marketing in a nutshell.

You usually do that by providing high quality, free content, solving people's problems, making them feel good about themselves, getting them involved around a cause they care about, and sharing content they will love (which is rarely, very rarely, ever YOUR content).

That's bad news for authors, because we can be selfish creative beings who aren't very interested in other people's problems. We may not even like other people that much. We may not really have anything to write about other than the books we are working on.

It's a little easier for non-fiction authors, because they are probably already in the information-sharing/problem-solving arena. For fiction authors, marketing in this scary, new, touchy-feely way seems backwards and trivial.

But I'm going to teach you how to do it.

Ready? I thought so.

As a warning, this guide is a short crash-course. I don't explore millions of different book promotion options. I also don't focus heavily on the nuts-and-bolts of book publishing or distribution—you can find that stuff out from other sources. This book is not about publishing, or putting your book up on Amazon or other sites. It's about selling a lot of books, building an author platform that can support your new career, and (ideally) making a full-time living.

Instead I lay out the elements of a strategy (or more properly, a "world-view") that you can count on to sell more books. I focus on the few things that really matter. Don't get distracted by all the people offering to promote and market your book for you; they may be helpful as supplementary efforts, but they won't overcome your failure to fix the common errors that many indie authors overlook (or deliberately ignore).

It takes a little work, and most of it can't be outsourced (although you may need professional help with some aspects of your marketing campaign, like editing your sales copy or designing your graphic elements).

On the other hand, something I'll stress in this book is that none of the details matter if you haven't established the basics.

As Dan Poynter (author of *The Self-Publishing Manual*) says:

The two secrets to book sales are:

1) **to produce a good product that has a market**
2) **to let people know about it**

As a full-time editor turned book cover designer, I have almost a decade of experience in *producing excellent products.* I know that a well-edited, well-formatted book with a brilliant cover will market itself, and everything you do will be a thousand times easier. So while this book isn't totally focused on publishing/book production, that doesn't mean it isn't important: "design" is a magic wand that super-charges your sales, and most indie authors are oblivious.

I also don't have any control over the subtle but pivotal factor Dan raised in his point #1: you need to write a book that **has a market.** Almost all indie authors write a book, and then try to find a market for it or make people read it. If you pour your soul into making your first book a success and it fails anyway, you probably wrote a book with no market—but now you can learn from your mistake and start writing books people want to read.

This is important, so I'll repeat it from another source. In *Kindle Bestselling Secrets,* Derek Doepker lists **Bestseller Secret #3**:

> "Average authors write a book and then ask, 'How can I make this a bestseller?' Bestselling

> authors ask, 'What book will become a
> bestseller?' and then write that book.

This is called by some, starving artist types, "selling out." By rich, successful authors, it is also called "selling out" as in, "Wow, my first print run of 10,000 copies *sold out!*" (If you don't feel comfortable viewing art as the creation of a product that you want to sell for money, then your ideology is prohibiting your success).

Planning for success by writing books that readers want to buy is *not a negative thing,* it's merely seeking to add value by caring about your readers. Average authors are on their own agenda. Bestselling authors are on their customers' agenda (This is Derek Doepker's **Bestseller Difference #2**). He explains,

> To embrace this mindset, I simply switch the
> question, "how can I get value?" to "how can
> I give value?" This could mean switching
> "how can I get more book sales?" to "how
> can I create a book so valuable that tons of
> people will naturally want to buy it."

This is the key to changing your limiting beliefs about art and writing. The idea that inspiration comes from your inner muse, and because you wrote something it's bound to be successful, is a *selfish belief.* If you want to be successful in business (and yes, writing and publishing books and *making money at it* is a business) then you need to focus on giving value to your customers, fulfilling their needs and making them happy.

Since you've probably already finished the book you want to market, this is one mistake it's too late to fix. If your book has a very small market (due to poor planning), it will probably never become a bestseller. However, let's assume your book has a market (even if a very small one) and is a good product (you still have control over this one—a professionally produced book with useful content or a pretty good story can still sell well).

Most of this book will be about Dan Poynter's second step: How to let people know about YOUR book, when there are MILLIONS of others. How to build a loyal tribe of passionate followers who love you and promote everything you do; how to put book marketing on autopilot so you don't really have to do very much; how to focus on the really big stuff that moves a ton of books, rather than a thousand garbage promotional tweets, and how to get the ball rolling downhill with one big push.

And most importantly, how not to be annoying and piss everybody off and end up sad and alone. Book marketing is about bringing people together, making other people feel good, not trying to get everybody to do you favors. If it's about you, you're being selfish. Cut it out. Never ask for favors. Nobody owes you anything. Make it about them.

I don't believe in the kind of marketing that has you running around doing big signings and radio appearances (unless the book is a non-fiction book meant to bolster your professional image, and you plan to make real money in speaking or other services).

Me personally, that stuff is too much work. I want to do a few simple things online, pay a little bit of money if I have to, and produce a media frenzy and blizzard of Amazon sales that lets my book sell comfortably without actually doing much promoting at all. Yes, it's possible.

Let's get started.

I hate those books that are obviously a bunch of blog posts taped together with an introduction; or the ones loosely arranged into lots of different sections with no overall narrative. So I've done my best to keep things organized and to present them in a way that makes sense. I promise not to abandon you or dump a whole bunch of data into a section without commentary.

But it's also difficult to find an optimal chronological order to the book marketing process. You need to be doing a whole bunch of things, pretty much at the same time. So I have used section headers to try and organize things by topic, but also put them in more or less a logical order with a beginning, middle and end. That said, there is definitely some overlap and repetition. You may notice me saying the same things over and over again. As a rule of thumb, the more times I say something, the more important it is. So if you skip over it the first three times, hopefully it'll sink in by the fourth.

UPDATE: Keep in mind, things change *very quickly* and this book was written at the end of 2013. I've updated it a bit, but I'm also always learning, testing and adjusting my strategies. Follow me online for updated material. Also, the ebook version of this book is more useful since it has lots of clickable links; if you need one of those just email me and let me know what format you need (mobi/epub).

When I started self-publishing a decade ago, I tried *everything* to market my books—awards, book shows, international rights, radio, email campaigns, contests, TV... it was difficult, and frustrating. But as I became more and more involved in the indie-publishing community as a book cover designer, editor, formatter and writer, I began to notice examples of book promotion campaigns done wrong, and a handful done really, really right. I also became fascinated with online business, marketing and sales, and began to research trends, tips and tricks from marketers of all kinds—the guys who are making *millions* with product launches, and shifting the opinions of *millions* of consumers with smart branding. These days I even fly to exotic international locations to meet up with some of the top sellers in the world and learn from them at exclusive internet marketing conferences.

Meanwhile, my own books (some written with pseudonyms) sell steadily and earn me a nice income. I've even been reviewed in major media and sold international publishing rights. I've learned a lot. **And now I'm going to share it with you.** But the rules are changing quickly, as the shifting sands of social media make traditional marketing strategies nearly obsolete.

If you're like me, you've read a bunch of other book-marketing guides and maybe found them light on actionable content and heavy on personal success stories and biography. I believe as you read through this book you'll become aware of at least several different and new ways to market your book that will produce *real value* for you. And since you only need to sell a couple extra books to earn the price of this one, I'm pretty confident that you'll be happy with it. (If you aren't, please ask for a refund rather than posting a negative review.)

THE BASICS

When authors ask me about innovative ways to market their books, I usually tell them to focus on the basics: make sure their book is good, and it's something people want to read. Make sure it's got a nice cover, has been edited and formatted. Make sure the Amazon page/sales page has a killer description that hooks attention and creates desire to read the book, and make sure there are about a dozen reviews on it (positive or negative doesn't matter so much as long as it's balanced).

And most authors ignore me and start marketing anyway.

There's a review of this book on Amazon, and it basically says the author didn't like my book because I suggest investing some money in making a good product - and because she hasn't made any money with her books, she feels that's bad advice. She's right: if you spend money making your book into a nice product, you aren't guaranteed to be successful. But here's the other thing: if you don't spend money making your book into a nice product, your chances of failure will be much higher, and you'll never know if you don't try. That said, all the tips and suggestions I advocate in this book will cost you hundreds of dollars less than the average publishing costs of the main self-publishing companies.

So let me slow down and make sure you understand this: if you have an unprofessional book cover, a mediocre book description, zero reviews, and you are trying to market your book, you are wasting your time and throwing your money away. This step cannot be skipped. You'll probably skip it anyway and skim down to the "marketing" stuff, because you think "Oh I've already done all that, it's fine. People like my cover. I wrote my description myself and I think it's pretty good. What's next?"

In *Sell More Books! Book Marketing and Publishing for Low Profile and Debut Authors,* Steve Miller cites a quote from Scott Monty, Ford Motor Company's social media chief.

"Don't fix the marketing first; fix your product. Once you've got a good product to talk about, the marketing's going to flow from that."

And that's not just for cars. Joanna Penn, in *How to Market a Book,* writes:

"Make sure that your book is amazing, and professionally edited with a professional cover design. Spend money on this because all the marketing in the world won't sell a crappy book."

How much does cover design matter? Recently I did a case study with 10 authors; I remade their book covers for free to see what kind of difference it would make on their sales. All of them saw sales *double immediately.* Whatever kind of marketing or promotion you're thinking about doing, there's no better investment than getting a nicer book cover.

It doesn't have to be expensive—you can get something simple and clean that works well. If you have the images you want to use, you can hire someone on fiverr.com to blend them together for you. You can even make a cover in MS Word that looks pretty good—I set up a huge package of DIY book cover templates to get you started (you can download the guide and some free samples at www.diybookcovers.com).

Book cover tips

This isn't a book cover design manual, but here are a few things you should know:

Strong colors and contrast is important. Teal to orange gradients work well.

Use complementary colors—red doesn't compliment anything but black and white.

A tagline or teaser, plus a review (or other small text) will increase sales.

It doesn't matter if you can read all the text as a thumbnail, it matters that it looks good.

Use simple, clean fonts, with lots of spacing—if you use a fancy or decorative font, only use one.

I wrote a couple of posts about book cover design recently (end of 2013) that got a lot of traffic, if you're designing your own cover, you might want to check those out (you can Google them).

<u>8 cover design secrets to manipulate readers into buying books</u>

<u>5 common book cover design myths most indie authors believe</u>

Formatting for Print and Ebook

I wasn't planning to talk about formatting the inside of your book, because how your book looks on the inside only matters post-sale. Except that Amazon readers can instantly look inside and will quickly scan to see if it's clean or ugly. Maybe you're still in the process and haven't figured out how to prepare your manuscript for print or ebook yet. So I may as well take a moment to deliberate—after all, a poorly formatted book or ebook can lead to bad reviews that will sabotage all your marketing efforts.

I learned to format ebooks from Unrulyguides.com, converting Word to clean HTML and then editing in Sigil. But it's a pain. You can use Calibre to make free ebook files but you don't have as much design control and the code can be buggy. Ebooks should be clean and functional, so don't get carried away on design or fonts or images... just make sure people can read it. I was excited to try Vellum to make ebooks but it's just for Mac. You can skip the whole process by using Smashwords or BookBaby; you can also find someone cheap to help you format or convert to ebook on fiverr.com (I'm going to reference fiverr.com a dozen times in this book, because I use it for everything.)

Your print book is a little harder. You can format your book in MS Word, but it can be *really* challenging to get everything done right. Joel Friedlander's Book Design Templates can help get you started, but if you can afford it, I'd pay someone to help. Having it done in Adobe InDesign will cost more, but the text and everything will look a little more professional. (If you hire someone, I recommend Lisa DeSpain.) Do the best you can, but if you do it yourself, be aware that it could probably look better and it's going to hurt sales.

While we're at it, if you haven't decided on a book editor yet, check out Paper Perfect Editing. You can send them a sample of your book, and several editors will get back to you with comments and changes so you can choose the best one for your book.

Your sales description

Having a strong sales description is critical also—pay to get it edited, these few paragraphs are your main "sales copy." They must convert browsers into buyers. Revise and test. Hire a copy writer.

You should also try to keep the text on your Amazon (or other sales page) neat and tidy by using bold text, italics and headings. You'll have to use some code; and it's a little different on the KDP (Kindle) site vs. the Author Central area. From what I understand (as of Nov. 2013) you can only use italics, bold and lists on Author Central, but can still use headings on the KDP site. Here's an article with more info on that from my friend Suzanne of *Unruly Guides*.

Note: I set up the KDP description for this book perfectly. But then I changed something on the Author Central page (not in the description, just my author bio). The Author Central version of the description took over, displaying very poorly. I contacted customer service and gave them the exact code - they used Author Central to plug it in, so it still looks bad, and so far I've been unable to get them to just use the version that's already on KDP and looks fine. Lesson: you may want to give yourself a few extra weeks before you're thinking of launching just to get the display formatting to work. Try to use Author Central as little as possible. Keep working with customer service until it looks great.

How to get HTML code to make your description look better? If you're a member, Author Marketing Club has an "Amazon enhanced description maker" that helps with your book's html listing, but I'm going to show you a couple of alternatives. The first is the online HTML editor from quackit.com. The page is cluttered and the menu looks overwhelming, but basically just click the "source" button on the top left, and it will change your text into HTML format that you can copy+paste into KDP's description field.

Another way you can do it if you're using Wordpress—just create a new post to type out your book description as you want it. Then look for the gray tabs on the far right that say "Visual" and "Text." If you switch to "Text"—it will show you the HTML version. You can copy+paste that code and use it for your book listing on KDP.

If you want to get even more creative, Michael Alvear's book <u>Make A Killing On Kindle</u> has some great tips about customizing your Amazon page for maximum sales.

Are you ready? Are you sure?

Don't just ask your friends and family—they are your own worst enemy. I've seen "friends" rave about how wonderful a cover design is, when it's really the worst I've ever seen. Good friends will support you and make you feel good—that's *not* what you need right now.

Instead, go on fiverr.com, hire some strangers to look at your book cover or edit your sales description. It's cheap. Improve each 10% and you'll get 20% more sales.

If you want more feedback on your book cover and sales description, send me a link to your book's Amazon page, you can email me here: <u>derekmurphy@creativindie.com</u>.

Checklist

- Amazing book cover
- Amazing, hot-selling Amazon description
- At least 10 reviews

Do you already have all of that? If so, you're ready to move forward. But keep this in mind: A book that's destined to be a success will grow naturally by word of mouth.

Take the *Wool* series by Hugh Howey. It started out as a short story with an extremely plain cover. The book's now enormous success has very little to do with Hugh's marketing and promotion strategies. It was a good story, and people liked it, so he wrote more. (But at the same time, his success wasn't accidental: Howey tried a few types of stories, listened to his readers, and finished the stories that they liked best.)

Listen to this quote about *Shades of Gray* in an interview with The Guardian newspaper:

Throughout January and February, sales grew at an absurd, unbelievable rate. It topped the Amazon erotica chart, then their general fiction chart, then entered the New York Times Bestsellers list and kept climbing. Emails demanded to know the name of the genius in charge of Erika's marketing campaign. There was no marketing campaign. Apart from a few book blogs, it was all word of mouth.

If you want to be a huge bestseller, write a great book in a very popular genre (erotica or post-apocalyptic fiction), and you won't need to do much marketing at all.

Some books sell more than others. Some are better written than others. You want to give your book its best chance at success, but promoting a poorly executed book, or a brilliant book that nobody wants to read, will turn you into literary Sisyphus—a perpetually frustrated author, trying to force people to read something they aren't interested in.

But let's assume your book has *some* value for *some* readers. What's the best, cheapest and most powerful way to get your book in front of *those* readers so that they can buy the book?

Let's start by building your author platform.

CREATING YOUR AUTHOR PLATFORM

What is your author platform? All the stuff online that collectively builds a portrait of you, the author. Why is it important? No matter what kind of marketing you do, that marketing will bring people back to Amazon or your website and based on what you've got posted, they'll decide whether or not to buy the book. We've already talked about having a great book, cover and sales description—but they will also look at your picture and read your author bio, so give it some love.

Many authors have trouble writing their own short bio, but your author biography matters because people can't really interact with an inanimate object like a book. Even if they love your story, they won't become a raging fan unless they connect with *you*. That's what it means to have an author brand—you need to invent a story of yourself that resonates with your target readers and gets them to *like* you.

And that's what building an author platform is about—getting people to know and like you, so they can make an emotional connection with you. The way to do that is by sharing a powerful author story: in other words, you need to summarize your life in the format of an emotional story that captivates the imagination.

Most good stories have a conversion or transformative event. As Bernadette Jiwa says in *The Fortune Cookie Principle: The 20 Keys to a Great Brand Story and Why Your Business Needs One*, a memorable narrative or personal story has a "pain point, a solution, a bad guy (the oligopoly), and a big goal."

Author Peep Laja writes, "Don't pitch your product, but the story of why it matters." Fiction authors may have trouble with this, because they want readers to love the story—they want the work to stand on its own. They don't want to focus the attention on themselves. And if the story is great and people love it, then the author bio won't matter as much. But you're trying to sell books to people who *haven't read the story yet*. In other words, the story can't sell itself before people have had a chance to read it.

So when you pitch the story, they may not be that interested. But if you pitch a meaningful author narrative, the "why" behind the writing of the story, it may have more clout.

Think of J.K. Rowling's author story—single mother riding on trains, writing in coffee shops while on food stamps. Is it true? Probably in part, but it's equally probable that a smart publicist focused on that narrative.

This is why, as *Kimberley Grabas* says on yourwritingplatform.com:

> *Before you do anything to promote yourself or your work, you MUST be able to articulate plainly, succinctly, and without hesitation: why you write what you write, and who cares that you write it. It's time to roll up your sleeves and dig deep into who you are, what you stand for, and why you create the work that you do—and for whom you are creating it.*

Gary Vaynerchuk, an expert on marketing (especially through social media) writes "Great marketing is all about telling your story in such a way that it compels people to buy what you are selling." He does this by trying new formulas, until he figures out how to best tell his story "in a way the audience *for that platform* wants to hear" (*Jab, Jab, Jab, Right Hook*). It's not about your PRODUCT. It's about connecting with people, but in a way that is OK for them. Why? If people land on your sales or Amazon page, then great—you don't matter so much. The product matters. But what marketing is really all about is trying to find and drive people to your product page. But why should they if they don't know you, or if everything you're doing is annoying and they want you to go away? Your product doesn't matter when you're marketing—YOU matter; how you present yourself, how you talk and communicate, how you make other people feel.

Most authors try to write a biography that's flattering, but it comes across as bragging or trumped-up. Unless you're writing a serious academic book where your credentials matter, nobody cares what awards you won or school you went to. But they *may care a lot* if you have two cats that you love, enjoy hiking and always sleep late on Saturdays. Why? Because you're creating a persona that's human, and that they have something in common with.

In "No Brand is an Island," Robert D. Smith suggests asking yourself seven questions to reach your *mission statement*. I won't share them all, but my favorites are:

Who would you like to become, and how will you know when you have become that person?

Who would you like to reach, and what specific impact would you like to have on them?

Write a few pages about that, then boil it all down to a few sentences (Robert suggests using only 140 characters!)

How to write an author bio that sells books

You can also organize your life with a big goal, an enemy (or challenge), and a conversion point. It doesn't have to be exactly true; you can play up an event to give it more meaning.

Then think about things that your readers like. Imagine your perfect reader: how can you let them know that you're just like them, that you have things in common? Be open, humble and human. It's OK to share your fears or doubts.

Mine goes something like this:

I used to believe I could be an author or artist just by producing the work I wanted to, by following my passion and intuition... but after spending years chasing my dreams, I was still poor and wasn't getting anywhere. That's when I realized to be successful, you have to make things that other people like, want or need. You have to help others. Since then, I've focused on being relentlessly helpful and everything has been so much easier.

And that's really not a great example. It's got to be shorter and more powerful. I'll probably hire a coach to work with me on it.

Your author bio matters, much more than you think it does, in building your author platform. And it's short. Pay a professional to edit it, someone who really knows what they're doing, not just any editor. **Update:** I'm actually working on a site totally dedicated to helping you fix your author bio or byline, but I'm not sure when I'll finish building it: www.roguebyline.com.

First person is better for your own blog, but 3rd person is probably better for Amazon, so you can focus on accomplishments without bragging. So while I talk about myself like this on my blog, "Hey there, I'm Derek Murphy. I help authors and artists make and sell their best work" I try to stick with this on bigger websites: "Derek Murphy is a writer and book cover designer studying his PhD in Taiwan..."

Get some professional headshots

You're also going to need a professional picture of yourself. People can't connect with an empty white box. Even if you're self-conscious about your appearance, make it happen. You don't need an expensive photographer (although it could help). Look on Craigslist for a photographer near you, or ask if any of your Facebook friends have a nice camera and want to come over for dinner and a photoshoot. You can get a nice effect by putting a normal standing lamp right next to you for that "studio" look.

Most smartphones can also take high enough quality pictures. Go to a bookshop and fake a book signing, or a park and try to get happy natural shots. If you're self-conscious like me, it may be hard to get a photo that looks really relaxed and natural (beer may help). Just do the best you can. Post your favorites on Facebook for feedback. (I'm not saying that you shouldn't hire a professional photographer if you can afford to... only that this is a necessary step and you've got to get it done. "I can't afford it" isn't an excuse.)

Ideally, you'll use the same author photograph everywhere, to build your brand. Something else you probably didn't know—people trust and like people they can see. That's why all cutting edge internet bloggers (who have something to sell) are making videos, usually a series of videos full of free advice and tips. Spending time watching somebody else talk builds a relationship and creates a sympathetic bond... which makes you more likely to buy what they're selling. (I'm sure some do it just to be helpful of course, but others do it because they know it will seriously impact their platform).

So you might think about recording a short "hello/welcome/about me" video you can use as well as your author photo.

Got your author story and picture?

Let's start using it.

Setting up your Amazon author page

A lot of authors start with social media profiles or a website but never update their Amazon Author page. While this isn't the most important part of your Amazon sales page, it matters, and some readers may click through. If you have no picture, no author page (or a poorly written one) you may have lost the sale. Go to the Amazon Author Central page and claim your book, and update your details with your story, links to your site or social media profiles, and author picture or video.

Setting up your author website

The first thing you should know about making an author website is that it can be a marketing black hole. It's very easy to get it wrong, so it can kill sales. If you spend money on marketing or advertising but the lead dies on your website, your book will never have a chance.

That's why it *can be more effective* to send people directly to a Facebook or Amazon page, because at least things will look good. It can also suck up a ton of money (if you pay several thousand dollars for your website) which you are unlikely to earn back, and time (if you obsess about small details, colors, fonts, positioning—rather than picking something easy that works).

And because I've seen so many awful author websites, I'm tempted to tell you to skip it, because it isn't worth the effort and money. But that's not really true either, for a few reasons.

As author William Hertling discovered when marketing his book with a targeted Facebook campaign, "People I sent to my landing page (his website) were twice as likely to purchase as people I sent directly to the Amazon page. The landing page was more effective at convincing visitors to purchase the book" (Indie & Small Press Book Marketing).

This is probably because even people who were marginally interested enough in the book to click the ad needed more convincing and information. They weren't ready to buy—so when they were taken to the Amazon page, they backed out. Whereas after spending a few minutes on William's website, they could read a bit about the book and the author without feeling pressured, and were more likely to buy the book.

But there's a bigger reason to make an author website: you need to create your own seat of power. You need to be able to control your relationship with your online connections. And most importantly, *you need to start an email list.*

As Tim Grahl writes in *Your First 1000 Copies:*

> "Your #1 goal as an author should be
> to grow your email list as much as
> possible. Write that on a post-it."

This is because nothing performs better than an email list for driving sales; people scan through Facebook posts and Twitter updates quickly, but almost everybody still opens almost all of their email.

Building an email list gives you the ability to build real relationships with people over time and be able to reach them when you have a new book or project.

But it won't work for everyone. In a little while I'll give you some tips for growing a list. While it's important and powerful, it may be difficult if you're a fiction author and can't find a way to offer more value than just the books you write.

Getting started with Wordpress

I like Wordpress because it's free, pretty easy to use, and can be very nice-looking. The default Wordpress themes, "Twenty-Twelve" or "Twenty-thirteen" are actually pretty stylish right off the bat.

You can throw in a nice header, a nice logo, and change the fonts with a plugin like Fontific or Google

Fonts. You can even change the background pretty easily. All of that takes about an hour, and you have a very decent website.

You can use a handful of plugins to display your book, buy now links, excerpts, an author bio and photo, and your social media profiles. You can sign up for free with Mailchimp for an email list and use a plugin for the sign-up box (a plugin is like a very small function that gives your Wordpress blog more options). I've put together a list of the best plugins to help authors sell books, you can read that here.

FREE GIFT

Recently I made a Wordpress plugin to increase traffic and social shares, developed with indie authors in mind. If you want a free copy, just go and subscribe on my site: www.creativindie.com

GET IT NOW FOR FREE

If you want to upgrade even more, you can search for premium Wordpress themes (I like themeforest.com, where most themes cost around $20).

If you have a bigger budget, you can take a look at Thesis or Genesis (very clean, nice Wordpress frameworks that allow for some child-themes). I'm not a fan of either because I think they are harder to customize and get used to, but many of the biggest bloggers use them because they are super clean, fast and functional.

Some other premium Wordpress template sites I like are: themefuse.com, elegantthemes, www.woothemes, and themetrust.

Best method: pick a theme you like the style of. Buy it, then hire a Wordpress designer on Elance to fix it up a *little bit.* You can get a header for $5 on fiverr.com.

You can even skip the header and use a font replacement to give the website name and subtitle some style. Save the pretty pictures for your book cover. Or have one nice landscape or abstract colors picture... but don't have a ton of different pictures on every page.

Likewise, slider headers are cool right now, but they probably won't help you. They're meant to display a lot of info fast—I use one on my covers site to show off a bunch of cover designs quickly. But you most likely have one book, a few pages, a simple blog. There's no need for a sliding header.

Don't get carried away, and don't change too much. Many authors admit they have no sense of style but then want to micromanage their website (or book cover) design and tweak everything. Keep it clean and simple. Less is more.

The secret of a successful author website

You need to decide what you want readers to do, and you need to make it easy and obvious for that to happen. This is called a "Call to action." If you want them to sign up on your list for a free sample or short ebook, make that the most visible thing on your site. If you want them to buy the book on Amazon, everything on your site should lead people to take that action. If you have a whole bunch of competing calls to action, they won't take any and will just leave the site.

Remember, you're trying to make a stranger do something. Why should they? A free book isn't a huge draw, especially if they need to jump through hoops to get it. Make it as easy as possible for them; make it a no-brainer.

Is your site ugly? Can it be better? Find out!

I stopped offering Wordpress sites for authors because many authors made poor choices and demanded changes that would have hurt their sales. Don't trust yourself, or your friends and family. Get real, professional feedback. Someone I use frequently to check my sites is Danielle ("liquiddragonn" on fivver.com). For $25 she'll check your website and give you solid feedback on what to improve.

What to write about on your website

If you do decide to set up an author website, you may spend weeks making it beautiful and then be stuck. After you've posted your Author Bio and About page, an excerpt and description of your book, some reviews, your book cover and a "Buy Now!" link to Amazon or wherever you want to send customers, what will you write about?

"SEO" is meaningless if you don't have any content— an old internet adage is: "content is king."

You need to write articles about things potential readers are searching for. In that light, setting up a website for yourself or your book may be a dead-end. You might be far more successful setting up a website about indie publishing, or a review site for books in your genre (where you can review the top bestsellers in your niche, bringing in the right kind of readers, and then having your book in the sidebar of every page).

You could write how-tos for other self-publishing authors. You could write tips on writing in your genre. You could write short stories or fiction. Identify what things your potential readers are interested in or want to read about or search for. Make a *larger* site that can become a hub for a community of readers, which your book appeals to. You will need to be creative to find topics.

Jonathan Gunson gives a good example in *Bestseller Labs*:

If you've written a fantasy novel about a warrior princess, then you could write a blog post entitled: 'The Top Four Warrior Women In Books & Movies', which would rank your favorite female warrior characters in popular culture. The post could then go on to discuss how one of these famous female characters was the inspiration for the lead character in your own book.

You can also comment on or tie into current events, news and celebrity issues. Bring up topics and characters that you know your readers will like. If you wrote a book about kids using magic, and your fans will probably also like Harry Potter, you could share interesting stories about Daniel Radcliffe.

If you wrote a futuristic technothriller, you could write about any innovative inventions or technology articles and what impact they may have on society's future. A great way to get ideas is to sign up for <u>Google alerts</u> based on keywords: Google will search the web for you and give you a list of matching articles and blog posts—some of these may be worth sharing or commenting on.

If you have content, people will find you naturally through Google searches. So when you write a timely follow up to a big issue, you could get thousands of visitors in a day. If you do it regularly and have a lot of content, you may get 10 or 20 thousand visitors a month—and if your book is right there on the sidebar (it should be) this will result in some sales. So writing blog posts = free, long-term marketing that will keep working indefinitely.

Some quick tips

- Numbered lists work really well.
- Snag with a headline, then start with a quote or personal anecdote
- Be (very) informative or entertaining.
- Show off your writing skills. Make each post great.

The trick is to engage and have a conversation with your readers—so try to end your blog posts with a question, "And what do YOU think about this...?" The conversation can continue into the comments. If the conversation gets big enough you might get some "trolls" (bored people who just like to be negative). It's up to you, but I have zero tolerance for trolls—I usually say "thanks for your comments but I want to keep this conversation positive!" or just delete their comments. Don't get riled up and begin an online debate. Never be negative online, it can only hurt.

Although you want to share your personality and let readers get to know you, writing about your day and trivial matters probably won't help: As the excellent blogging resource *Copyblogger* writes:

"Let's not pussyfoot around it. The harsh truth is this: Your readers aren't interested in you, your life, or your stories. As a blogger and content marketer it's your job to help your readers, to guide them, and inspire them. Talking about your experiences is fine—it can add color and personality to your posts—but only if it helps your readers become healthier, happier, or more productive. When you want to write a story about your life, ask yourself this: What's in it for my readers? How can my experience help them?" (11 Common Blogging Mistakes That Are Wasting Your Audience's Time).

When you start blogging, you'll also want to share a sample of your book or excerpt. You may be worried about how much free content you should share. Tim Grahl has this response:

Obscurity is the enemy that you should be worried about above all others. Therefore, hiding everything you create until it's bound together in a book is not a smart idea; you will be quite lonely when you start looking for readers once the book is published. The solution is to share, and share widely. And deeply. And too much (Your First 1000 Copies).

How often should you blog?

Once or twice a week would be enough, except it would take you a year just to have less than 100 articles. You may want to write more in the beginning—try to get 10 amazing articles on your blog right away, along with really well written main pages (about, excerpts, reviews, sales summary). Once you have that many, you can start guest posting or driving traffic back to your site.

If all this sounds too difficult for you, and you aren't able to think of creative ways to link your book's topic with current events or news, then having your own website may not really do much marketing for you. If that's the case, you can still use your website as a "base" but it will be less effective. Try to post at least once a month just so Google doesn't forget about you.

Building your email list with an opt-in offer

Internet marketers have a saying, "The money is in the list." But the list only works if you find people who are interested in your writing. They give you permission to contact them in exchange for something you're offering on your site. This will be tricky for fiction writers—what do you have that you can give away? Numbered lists make very good opt-in offers, maybe something like:

- The 10 most common grammar error writers make
- 12 excellent ways to make your hero more likeable
- The 50 best written fiction introductions of all time

Offering a sample of your writing or free book won't work *unless* you're already hooked them with free samples. If it were me, I'd put a very powerful passage on my homepage to grab attention right away, and give them enough to get into the story. Then at the end, I'd say "Want to read more? Sign up on my mailing list and I'll send the first 3 chapters, or you can buy it online now!"

I should point out at this point something I've so far omitted: the easiest and best marketing is having a lot of books. If you're trying to market just one book, everything will be harder. Not impossible, not unworthy of attempting, just harder. Which means you'll need to work more and be more patient, and have lower expectations for the success of your book. If you have a series of books that begins with a short story, that can be your free giveaway.

If you only have one book, you can still try to think of an opt-in offer, but having a list won't do you much good (what do you need the list for, if you won't have more future books to sell later on?) If that's the case, rather than trying to build an email list, you'll probably just want to drive book sales and get reviews. So you could use your website to focus on those instead. Remember, you want just one call to action, so don't ask them to do too much.

If doing all that seems unmanageable right now and you're not ready to get started, you may do better without a website and just focus on your Amazon and other bookseller sales pages (where you can also make an author page, but everything will look nice).

Getting initial reviews

At this point, we're still just setting up shop. Many authors make the mistake of trying to sell their book before their platform is ready; but even if your book and website look great, people may still be reluctant to trust you. This is where "social proof" or reviews come in. You need to get as many reviews as you can, hopefully at least ten, before you start doing any serious marketing.

But how do I get reviews? You say. It's tough, I know. Giving out copies to your friends and family doesn't work as well as it should, and sometimes puts them in an uncomfortable position between their integrity and their loyalty to you. You can buy some if you have to (paid reviews do not equal "fake" reviews; they can be both professional and honest, like Kirkus or Foreword, although I wouldn't pay that much for a review.) You can also nag the hell out of a few people until they post something.

To start, make a list of 30 to 40 or so *dream people* who may review your book. Oprah is probably busy, but other authors in your field, other indie bloggers or indie book review blogs, leaders in your community or minor celebrities, local newspapers, your local library... Get their emails and ask them for reviews. Check in with them politely at least 3 times before you give up. Yes it's humbling, humiliating, and potentially annoying. Try not to be too obnoxious. Here are a few sample letters you can use:

#1: Hi _____, I'm a big fan of your work and what you're doing in the community, I noticed you recently reviewed _____. I'm also an author and am just wrapping up a book on _____, which is similar. I think you may enjoy it, and would love to offer you a free copy. It's about (*very brief, 1 or 2 powerful sales sentences that sell your book*). Of course a review or blurb would be welcome if you have the time and you feel you can honestly endorse my book, but I will totally understand if you're too busy right now for that. Still, I'd like you to have a copy just in case, so please send me a quick reply with an address I can ship it to. Thanks! Sincerely,_____

#2 (send 3 days later) Hi again, I just wanted to follow up and make sure you got my earlier email. Did you get a chance to read it? I'm just hoping I can send you a review copy of my book _____, which is about_____(even briefer summary____, like I said, no strings attached, I just wanted you to have a copy to thank you for being inspirational to me.

Thanks, _____

#3 (send 3 days later) Dear _____, I know you're busy and I don't want to be a nuisance, but just in case you aren't getting my emails or have been on vacation I thought I'd try one last time to get in touch with you regarding my book _____. Getting a review from you would be a dream come true and I want to make sure I've tried my best before giving up. So if you think you may have time to look it over in the next few months, on the condition that a review is completely optional and it's no big deal if you end up not having enough time, I'd still like to send you a copy. Thanks, Sincerely_____.

If you're "cold-calling"—or approaching a stranger for a book review, at least the above letters are polite and professional. **But they still probably won't work.** You'll be much more successful if you target the people you want to review your book, follow them on Twitter and Facebook, interact with them for a few months and provide value. Then, once they know who you are, send a very short and very casual message to them. I'll talk more about using Facebook and Twitter to build these relationships later.

It's also a good idea to build upwards. Don't shoot for the top in the beginning—first find a few friends and casual readers to review your book. Then aim a little higher, at small blogs. The bigger the fish, the more reluctant they will be to endorse your book, so you should already have established social proof and value before you contact them. (At that point, if you want to be bold and they are ignoring your emails, send a copy of your book and a handwritten note with a clever gift— something you know they will like. It may not work... but it could open the door).

Don't ask for good reviews

One of the biggest barriers to getting good book reviews is the *expectation of positive feedback*.

Authors don't really want reviews—they want good, five star reviews. But this expectation puts a lot of pressure on reviewers, especially if they feel like they can't be honest with their opinions about the book. So if you're asking them for a positive review, you may be asking them to lie. *Why should they?* Indie authors can also be unprofessional and over-sensitive to negative reviews, so rather than risk starting an online feud, most people will just ignore you and not return your emails.

The way to overcome this is to recognize that positive reviews don't matter: Most people ignore them anyway and go for the 2 or 1 star reviews. Having a bunch of reviews just means a lot of people are reading the book. You should try to maintain at least a 3-star average, but even this can't really be controlled. If you're asking for reviews, make it clear that you don't expect reviewers to give false or fake reviews, and that you'll be grateful for any honest feedback they post, even negative.

This may sound horrifying to you, but if you're scared of negative reviews, then your book isn't good enough, and it's better to find that out early rather than sinking a ton of money into promotion first. Ask for honest feedback. Never respond to negative reviews with anything more than silence, or perhaps. "Thank you for the review." Don't get angry. Cool off. Focus on getting more positive reviews (people will review you more favorably if they like you, so positive reviews are the result of the relationships you're forging).

Often negative reviews are the result of connecting with the wrong readers, who expected something different. If your book looks like a YA romance, and you advertise on sites with lots of teenagers, and your protagonist is actually a widower kindling a steamy relationship with her gardener, you're going to get some ugly comments. It's not a problem with your book— it's a problem with your marketing. If you revise the cover, make the sales description clearer and focus on connecting with the right kind of readers, you'll see much more favorable feedback.

For that reason, make sure your book isn't too mysterious. You don't want people to buy it on a whim and hate it—you want to let the right readers know what it's about, and have proper expectations, so that those expectations can be met, rather than disappointed.

How to get more free reviews

We'd all like to get natural reviews from the people who buy our books, but only about 5% of book buyers leave reviews, and many people only leave reviews if they either love or hate the book. That means that you'd have to sell 100 books to get 5 reviews, and when you're just starting out, it's tough to get that first 100 sales - especially if you don't already have some reviews!

So unless you have an amazing, life-changing book, natural reviews that sell your book are really hard to come by.

In _How to Get a Truckload of Amazon reviews,_ Penny Sansevieri recommends pitching top amazon reviewers who reviewed similar books, and using the following Google search string to track them down:

Top 500 reviewer" + Romances + E-mail site:

http://www.amazon.com/gp/pdp/profile

Penny's other tips are to personalize each email, write thank yous, and keep active on sites like Goodreads.

Greg Pietruszynski of the _Growth Hacking Blog_ wrote this article recently that tells you how to pull anyone's email address from Twitter. (Which is brilliant, so that after you've interacted with them on Twitter and shared their content about a dozen times, you can email them and they'll know who you are.)

Another tool I've just started using (and think is amazing) is the "reviewer-grabber" feature in Author Marketing Club. You can search for a similar book on Amazon and the tool will hook you up with the email addresses of all the people who reviewed that book.

Keep in mind that they probably get a lot of review requests, and there's absolutely nothing in it for them, so you really are asking a big favor. At least make your pitch fun or interesting. (You could also offer a $25 Starbucks or Amazon card, which may incentivize some, but alienate others... it would be better to get the review first and then send a thank you card afterwards). On that note—if someone DOES review your book, please send them a nice, personalized thank you note. Thank them publicly on Twitter for being so awesome and generous.

Finally, you should check out <u>Story Cartel.</u> You give a copy of the book away and readers are encouraged to share their reviews. It's easy and will probably get you some extra reviews at no cost. (You have the option of adding a giveaway to encourage reviews, either 5 print copies of your book, 3 $10 Amazon giftcards or a Kindle.)

For my first book, I mass emailed everybody offering an iPad prize. It didn't work. People don't want to be bribed to read a book. They want to read a book because it's good. I also contacted a ton of bloggers and was lucky enough to have about a dozen get back to me.

The way I get free book reviews these days is to offer a huge prize (like a one week resort vacation) to the review voted most helpful on Amazon by a certain date (which gets lots of people to leave a review, and then tell their friends to go and vote their review 'most helpful').

But I can only do this because I've built up an email list by giving away a lot of valuable, free information and tools.

Still stuck for reviews? Organize a local "self-published author" club and command everyone to review each other's books—it will benefit everyone in the group. They don't have to be good reviews, or long reviews. You just need some. Make that your goal before doing anything else.

Update: For my new book, *Write, Format, Publish, Promote* I emailed my list an offer (free membership to DIY Book Covers) in exchange for a review - I got 35 reviews posted in one week, in time for my KDP promotion.

Why should anyone review your book for free?

Recent book review scandals have made everyone sensitive about the topic of paid book reviews. They have been branded as untrustworthy, false, fake, misleading, and just pure evil.

So *I understand* that the idea of paid book reviews might "rub you the wrong way." You can choose to get angry about it and ignore this section completely, and that's fine. It's not my responsibility to *convince you* to use any of these tips, I'm only offering things that work for authors who want to sell more books. Because nobody wants to pay for book reviews, tens of thousands of indie authors are sending out copies of their books to everybody and pleading their friends, relatives, strangers and online book reviewers to review their books. And if they can't get any, they give up (and their books languish, unread, unloved, because nobody wants to take a chance on a book with too few reviews).

Since this current state of affairs is extremely disadvantageous in regards to book marketing, serious writers need to be willing to re-evaluate their opinions and make more of an effort; specifically, they need to think more about what reviewers are really sacrificing when they do you the huge favor of reviewing your book, and how you might be able to compensate them.

Let's assume you have a medium sized book and it takes a few hours to read. With writing and posting the review, let's say it takes an average of 5 hours to review your book. (You don't want them to just skim, do you?) So when you're asking someone for a book review, you're asking for **five hours** of their time.

That's not a small favor. At minimum wage that's about $40. If you sent out a bunch of emails to people you didn't know and asked, "Hey I need a favor, can you give me $40?" how many replies would you get?

How many friends or relatives would fork over the cash, or 5 hours of their time? I'm lucky to have a bunch of people I can count on to support me, but I'd never ask them to do me this big a favor. If I needed five hours of someone's time, I'd pay for it.

Asking friends or family for reviews puts them in an awkward position. Not everybody is going to feel comfortable summarizing a whole book into a finely-tuned paragraph and publishing it publicly. On top of the five-hour theft of their time, you're probably pushing them out of their comfort zone. Why put that kind of strain on your relationships? Also, their reviews may steer clear of much-needed criticism, in order to spare your feelings.

And it's no better to ask for free book reviews from total strangers. Sure, some book review blogs make money from ads or services, and they review your book for free because it gives them content, which means more traffic, which brings in more money. But why should anybody else?

Offering them a free book? Who cares, they probably don't want it. Offering a $10 Amazon card? That's nice but not really enough. I just had someone ask me for a book review - I said sure, want to review mine in exchange? They wrote back saying they weren't really interested in my book. Why would I give away my time doing a stranger a favor when they aren't willing to do the same for me? (This doesn't mean that you should demand to trade reviews. If you want a review from another author, review their book first, no strings. Be proactive about giving other people reviews as a way to connect with them, expecting nothing in return, and it will probably pay off).

Buying or Trading reviews

Getting reviews for your book in the beginning will be difficult. Remember we're still not really marketing, we're just building relationships and making friends. But you want to have some reviews on your book's page immediately, and you don't want to put pressure on your budding online relationships by asking them to review your book (because later, when you do a *real* book launch, you're going to want them to help share it.)

So personally, I'd rather pay for book reviews. I think it's completely possible to get honest, genuine reviews from people and reward them for their time. I've used fiverr.com to find book reviewers. I tell reviewers I want them to be 100% honest, even if it's critical or negative. A simple, one or two sentence, genuine opinion is better for sales than a lengthy, in depth book review. Paying for *honest reviews* is the responsibility of the author. (I understand this is controversial - and I don't actually need to pay for book reviews now that I've built my platform. But if the alternative is having zero reviews and not doing anything about it, waiting for sales to happen which will lead to natural reviews, any marketing you do will be wasted. You *must* get reviews posted quickly before you get sales).

But Amazon now is removing anything suspected of being a paid review, and they are also deleting reviews from competing authors (which is frankly ridiculous):

> "We do not allow reviews on behalf of a person or company with a financial interest in the product or a directly competing product. This includes authors, artists, publishers, manufacturers, or third-party merchants selling the product. We have removed your reviews as they are in violation of our guidelines. We will not be able to go into further detail about our research."

But you could post an offer of $20 / review on Craigslist or your Facebook page. You could ask to edit or proof the reviews, but that's already shady territory and most reviewers won't feel comfortable with it. Most strangers will be tough but fair, and if you're overly sensitive and defensive, you're not ready to be publishing.

Even though Amazon is deleting reviews by competitors, you can still trade and post blurbs in the "editorial reviews" section. Always give before asking, so don't say, "Hey do you want to trade reviews?" or "Will you review my book if I review yours?"

Instead, buy 30 books that are similar to yours by other indie authors (big league authors probably won't respond). Read their books and post a review, then email them personally with, "Hi there, I just wanted to tell you I loved your book and just posted a review on Amazon. I put out a book that's kind of similar recently and I know how hard it can be to get reviews. I hope your book is really successful, it's really great!" (By the way, I'm building a handful of book review sites for exactly this purpose, join my list if you want the insider details on how to participate.)

Tell them the name of your book (or drop it accidentally in your email signature) but don't link to it or encourage them to go check it out. (Don't *ask* for anything. Just put yourself on their radar and build up the balance of social karma in your favor.)

In an ideal world, there would be a perfect online platform/system for trading honest reviews. I gave it my best shot recently with **www.BLURBTRADE.com.** It lets you connet with authors in your genre interested in trading book blurbs; giving blurbs to other authors not only can bring in more book reviews but is also excellent marketing in itself - anyone who sees that book will also see your blurb and want to find out more about you.

Note: once you start connecting with your target readers, and finding people who really like your book, getting genuine reviews should be much easier. "Fake" positive reviews you bought won't compensate for authentic negative reviews, so "cheating" isn't really an option. All I'm suggesting is to solve the "chicken-and-egg" problem, by getting a handful of reviews up right away, so that readers feel more confident about taking a chance on your book and can make up their own minds about it.

Something you also may want to look over is 1starbookreviews.com, which claims that negative book reviews can actually sell more books than positive ones.

Kindle vs. Print

I think you should start selling the ebook to build some reviews and get feedback, then when you put out the paperback and link both versions (Amazon should do this automatically) the page will already have some reviews - that's when I'd do a bigger launch or free book campaign. You'll get more results from a page with reviews and great sales copy, so you can start tweaking/building your Amazon page while you finish the print book, then when you're sure everything is good, you can launch harder. But some people say having the print version available will sell more ebooks, just because it looks more professional. At this point it doesn't matter so much because we're *not marketing*. We don't want a bunch of traffic. We are building a sales platform that will work.

And now you're ready to begin

The topics we've covered so far need to be handled before you really begin telling people about your book. You're establishing authority and credibility. You're getting your sales funnel set up. This is your basic platform. What you need to do now is test it out to see whether it actually works, and fine-tune it.

I'd like to introduce a few key terms of contemporary online marketing, and suggest ways for you to use them to sell more books.

The first is Conversion

Conversion means, out of all the people that found your website, your Amazon page, a book review—out of all the people who had your book right in front of them— how many actually went ahead and placed an order. 5%? 10%? This percentage is critical.

Most authors try to get more reach and visibility—and that's all they think about. But some authors are dealing with a **zero percent** conversion rate, which is like a black hole sucking up all your efforts.

Example One

Let's say you have an ugly cover, an amateur website with gifs of your dogs dancing, a book about your family vacation that you formatted yourself, and zero reviews (or worse, two five star rave reviews you wrote yourself). Let's say you had a few sales from your friends and neighbors after messaging them repeatedly on Facebook.

But then the sales died off. When somebody accidentally finds your book, they run away in terror. An author who doesn't know much about business may say, "Nobody is buying my book! I need to market it more!" So they spend money on advertising or book promotion. But with that zero percent conversion rate, they are throwing money away.

Example Two

Now let's say you're a run of the mill author with an OK book, a cheap book cover design (not horrible, but not so great), pretty nice formatting (that was done in Microsoft Word). You're selling about 10 books a month. You have about 10 nice, unsolicited reviews. You're about average, in a field with millions of competitors. Should you start marketing?

Well, that depends on your conversion rate, and how much it would profit you. Let's assume that, if you spend money on book marketing, you'd like to make it back in sales. If you make $1 per sale, a $100 advertising budget should lead to 100 sales.

A $100 advertising budget on Google or Facebook Ads (I'll suggest some alternatives later) might put your book in front of 10,000 people (actually it can be much more). But mostly people will ignore the ad completely (unless you do something more creative than advertising—but at this point we're not trying to drive a lot of traffic, we are trying to test things out).

Let's say 1000 people click the ad, and you get your 100 sales.

That means you have a 10% conversion rate, which is actually pretty good.

But it also means that advertising (at the rates I just suggested) will only allow you to break even.

That might be OK—if you spend $10,000 and get 10,000 sales, you'd earn your money back, get a bunch of reviews and a lot of exposure. At that point you could stop advertising and hopefully the sales would continue.

But if your conversion rate was 5%, you'd be losing money. And if your conversion rate was 20%, you'd be doubling the money you spent on advertising!

What if you're not advertising?

You should be. There are lots of options. Unlike a press release, interview or newspaper review, online advertising allows you to track your conversion rate—and it's important, so you should figure it out.

The easy way is with Google or Facebook ads, because they will give you a lot of data like exactly how many people clicked on the ad. But you can also put an ad on another blog or website's sidebar (either paid or for free) for as little as $20 a week (or even a month).

Try to do only one advertising method per week, so you can measure the increase in sales (if you have a website and you use Google analytics or a WordPress analytics plugin, you can see the amount of traffic increase you got, and compare that to sales, giving you a conversion rate).

Example: my book's website usually gets 100 people per day. I run a 2 week ad on a much bigger blog, that I've chosen because its readers are likely to enjoy my book. For those 2 weeks I get 150 people per day (incidentally, this means I'm getting 50 "clicks" per day and probably not paying much for them. It can be cheaper to test out an ad this way, rather than on Google, where the ad will show up anywhere).

During those two weeks I make 5 sales a day ($5 a day). So my conversion rate is only 3%. That's not great… however in 2 weeks I've made $70. A two week ad placement may cost much less than that. Let's say I only paid $20. Now, even though my conversion rate is low, I'm still making money. I'd probably keep that ad and try another somewhere else.

How to improve your conversion rate

Step One: I'll start with the easiest way. If you are paying for clicks, rather than impressions, you don't want people to click your ad unless they are likely to be serious buyers, because otherwise they're wasting your money. So you don't want an ad that appeals to everybody. You don't want it to be vague or unclear, or just say "Bestselling new book available now!"

You need to *qualify your leads*. This means getting rid of the ones that won't like your book. You do this with detail. A good ad will hint at the genre, setting, and major conflict. Focus on getting the text right first. Don't say stuff like "Bestselling Amazon Author." Instead hook their attention, use social proof with a nice review, tell them what the book is about (alien cowboy shoot-em-up, New Zealand wartime Romance, etc). Make sure they know what to expect before they click.

Then, those people who like that type of book, and *only* them, will click through to your site. The total number of visitors may drop, but they will be more likely to buy (as long as you follow through with a well-designed and well written sales page).

If you're not paying per click—for example you place an ad for $20/week—you don't need to qualify leads this way. You could just try to get a lot of traffic, perhaps be more vague, and hope they will buy even if they aren't really that interested. Either way, qualifying leads is a good place to start improving your conversion rate.

Step Two: Once you have a baseline conversion rate in mind (you're pretty sure, based on your traffic and sales, how many visitors become buyers) you can start improving your sales page. Most author websites are terrible. I'm not saying yours is, but the vast majority are, so you might want to take another look. Actually, you should get a stranger to take a look—go on fiverr.com and hire someone to go review your website and give critical feedback. Do it right now.

Improving the design of the website so it doesn't scare people away can help a lot. Start with that. Then, work on the content: is your book description and sales page set up in a way that makes people want to buy? Copy-writing is an art and a science. Learn it or hire someone. Just because you wrote a book doesn't mean you can write the 300 word sales description that stirs up an intense desire to buy the book.

You can avoid this step—and maybe you should—by ignoring your author website for now and just linking your ads to your Amazon sales page. There's much less for you to control on your Amazon sales page: your description, your reviews, and your book cover. Those three things are responsible for your conversion rate, so I'd focus on them first, make sure they're all working for you really well, before you waste months (as most authors do) fiddling with your website.

Split-testing

If you're trying to improve your conversion rate, it's hard to say what element of your sales page is broken. As I suggested earlier, paying someone to take a look is a good start. They may be able to point out some major flaws. But after that, you need to test different elements by making small changes at a time.

Can't decide on a cover design? Test out more than one. Your cover is the face of your book and directly linked to conversion and sales. Many authors choose a cover they like over one that would sell better. This is your prerogative and you can make your book however you want. But if you want people to read it, share it, buy it... make sure you get a cover that sells, not necessarily the one you like the best.

I always recommend my authors show the book to a lot of people to do some testing. Often they come back and say "I've shown it to 10 people and this is what they like." Asking people you know for feedback on your cover design is basically worthless. Try to get at least 100 votes, and make sure the margin is wide (70 to 30, rather than 40 to 60). But a more reliable way is to put up one cover for a week, then change covers, and see what effect (if any) it had on sales. This issplit-testing. To dosplit-testing well, you really need a lot of traffic. Measuring the actions from a few dozen people doesn't mean much. Try to get 1000 visitors before you analyze the data. Use bitly.com to generate shortlinks to your Amazon site if you want to know exactly how many people are clicking on your ads (valuable for measuring Amazon traffic, which is otherwise difficult).

Two different but comparable cover designs may not make a huge difference in sales, as long as they are both well done and look professional—but it's worth testing. Use split-testing to tweak your sales description too, which can always be better. Make it amazing. If you aren't selling and you don't have reviews, *that's* your problem—get more.

So let's say you've done all of this, and you are pretty sure your conversion rate has been improved, and hopefully is up around 20% (although 10% is still not too bad). Now you're ready to move on.

An easy way to make ads

That last section was pretty technical... if it was overwhelming, ignore it. The idea was to pay for *some* traffic, so that you could figure out how much of your traffic is actually buying the book, and to do it before you invite the whole world back to take a look at your website or Amazon page (because if it's still unpolished and unprofessional, you'll have just blown your *one chance* to make a good first impression.)

You can hire someone on fiverr.com to make a simple ad for your book. If you want to use your cover design, it may be fine *if it's good*. Here's another simple trick that you can use to make powerful ads. Get a friend or relative to let you use their Facebook chat and send yourself a message, something like "Hey, have you seen this book yet? It's getting good reviews on Amazon, seems interesting..." Then add the cover image and send it. You'll need a "screenshot" software like Snagit, (or else you can click Ctrl+PrtScn) to take a picture of your message and crop the image.

The trick is to keep it very casual so it seems authentic (even though they'll quickly realize it isn't "real," ads like this often outperform other examples).

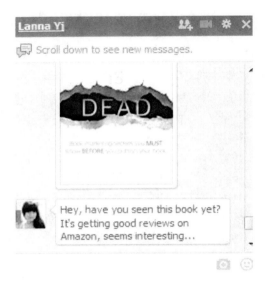

BUILDING SOCIAL KARMA

All the stuff up above is necessary to get started: you must have a firm foundation, a good looking, professional platform, to have a chance of success. Not having it is like trying to fill a leaky bucket full of water. But it's also not terribly effective at selling books, and on its own, it may not do much for you at first. This is because you don't have the power of trust: nobody knows you and trusts you personally (well, maybe a dozen or so people, but that isn't much). Which means, everything you're doing—no matter what kind of campaign or publicity, is a cold call. It's like knocking on someone's door and saying "Hey do you have a minute to talk about my new book?!" Nobody is going to let you into their house. No matter how well you're dressed or how much you smile or how loud you yell. They don't know you, so they won't trust you.

Effective book marketing *demands* you spend some time building relationships—and not fraudulent "I'll scratch your book if you scratch mine" business trades, but *real friendships*. (I just realized the error of the last sentence but I'm going to leave it in, maybe "Scratch your book" will become a new catchphrase.) You need to get people to know about you, and *like you*—and you can't do that trying to promote your book, or yourself.

But you can do it, and I will teach you some tricks to build up powerful relationships quickly and without much work or time investment. This section assumes that you've followed through with Stage One: if you still have an ugly book cover, a poorly written book description and author bio, or an unprofessional photo, networking will be much harder.

Getting Social

Because I operate in self-publishing circles, I have a lot of authors and author services on my Twitter feed. Depressingly, I'd say about 90% of authors I come in contact with come off as spammy self-promoters. Even more depressingly, the author marketing services, author networks and self-published book promoters come off the same way. (And these are the people that are taking authors' money to do promoting for them.)

There's a very simple rule: 90% of your content should not be about yourself or your book. You should be sharing other people's posts, researching and finding useful information online, helping people solve problems, and making positive relationships by providing value.

I know authors who tweet about their book 20 times a day, each time trying to use a clever new twist, sale, giveaway, prize or description (and more recently, posting sexy images... which is actually a big improvement to their marketing).

Advertising takes repetition: if you are paying to advertise, people may see your ad 25 times before finally wondering what it's all about and clicking the link.

But social media is not advertising

Spammy, self-promotional posts may seem to work in the indie community, because everybody is doing it and indie authors support each other, but you're not reaching the much broader market of *everybody else*.

Everybody else is made up of savvy consumers who got used to sales-speak and are cynical, hesitant and skeptical. They won't trust you when you tell them your book is awesome.

This is why, during Stage Two, **you shouldn't be marketing.** You are trying to establish trust and make friends. And you can't do that by selling or marketing your book. Instead, you need to be useful, friendly and helpful.

"Being useful, helpful and generous is satisfying to you personally, but also builds up a bank of goodwill. When you later mention that you have a book out, or people are attracted to you because of your generosity, and see you have books/products available, they are more likely to buy." (Joanna Penn, *How to Market a Book*)

"Relationship marketing deals with selling second and building relationships first. Where old-school marketing focuses on clever or salesy ways of convincing people to buy what you are selling, relationship marketing focuses on creating a connection with your audience so that they come to know, like, and trust you. Demonstrate that you care about people first and making money second, and your business will grow." (D'vorah Lansky, *Book Marketing Made Easy*.)

"Become a beacon of enhancement, and then when the night is gray, all of the boats will move toward you, bringing their bountiful riches." (James Altucher, *Choose Yourself!*)

"Are you making your customers feel a part of something, happy, or loved?" (Jiwa, Bernadette, *The Fortune Cookie Principle*.)

"Marketing is two things: (1) creating
lasting connections with people through
(2) a focus on being relentlessly helpful"
(Tim Grahl, *Your First 1000 Copies*).

You'll basically have two levels of relationships: The people with connections have large followings because they've built up trust—and they're not going to betray that trust by sharing or recommending anything that isn't absolutely incredible.

And everybody else, who are eager to network and will repost just about anything if they think it will get them some currency with the real influencers. And of course, once people begin reading your book, you'll start to build a community of your own fans and followers, but that comes later.

Right now, you want to make lots of friends, but most importantly, you want to make a few close friendships with some powerful bloggers or community leaders. These are the gatekeepers. One tweet from them could sell thousands of your book. But there's no way they're going to help you promote your book unless they really know, like and trust you.

Luckily, it's pretty easy to make friends with important people: here's the secret. They get contacted ALL the time by people asking for stuff. So whenever anybody new comes on their radar, comments on their article, sends them an email, says nice things about them, they are skeptical. They are waiting for the other shoe to drop, and ask themselves, "What's this person want from me?" And most of the time, they're right. So don't be another one of those people asking for something. Think about what you want from them, what would be awesome (a review or an article about your book) but don't ask for it!

Instead, find a way to help them. Share their content. Review their stuff. Give critical feedback. Interact. Do this for a while (several months ideally, but at least a couple weeks) until they get to know who you are. If you can, find a way to meet them in person (at an event or conference) or sign up for their online seminar or class (even if it's expensive, the connection may be worth it.)

First steps

There are lots of social media sites, but for making relationships, you should focus on Twitter, Facebook and Linkedin. There are other sites we'll start using later, during the marketing section (Stage Three).

Make a list of 25 influential people online who you'd love to be friends with; people with large followings who you like and respect. If you can't think of 25, do some research. See who other people follow. Go to their blogs and read a bunch of their articles. Get to know them.

Find out what they love and hate. Find out what they enjoy and what they find difficult or challenging. Find out where they live, what hobbies and skills they have.

Yes, it's kind of like stalking. But it also shows you actually read their content. You don't want to be another one of those jerks who emails them and says "Hey, I see you have a lot of followers. I don't know anything about you myself, and I haven't read any of your material or blog posts, but can you share my new book?"

You need to know something about them so that you can interact with them more genuinely, and more easily. You won't have to think hard about what to say, because you kind of "know them" already after having spent time reading their material. You get their humor and personality. Which means you can treat them like a regular human being, rather than a cold, stiff and awkward stranger.

Tip: I had a lot of trouble getting into Social Media until I got an iPhone. The mobile version of the following websites eliminate a lot of confusing choices, and make things easier. Plus I use it a lot more often, whenever I'm away from my computer and have time to kill. Something to consider if it all seems "overwhelming."

How to use Twitter to make friends

When you sign up at Twitter, I recommend you use your real name rather than a business or publishing name. I use "@creativindie" which is good for brand recognition, and my name shows up if anyone checks my profile, but basically you want to be a human on Twitter. So having a real name and your awesome author photo are a good start. You'll need to shorten your author bio to fit Twitter's length allowance; add a short description and a link to your website or book.

Twitter software services

There are a bunch of software and services that help you manage your Twitter better. I recommend not using any. Is it easy? Yes—but it's also less personable. I get automatic messages when I follow someone with software, like "Thanks for the follow! You might also want to check out my new book...." but I ignore them, because they're breaking the first rule: never market to someone you've just met. (Although, you could say "If you want a *free* copy of my new book, you can get it here.") The word "Free" can make someone interested in something they otherwise wouldn't have had time for.

Add your list of influences, and anybody else you like. You can also search Twitter for hashtags or keywords. Should you follow everyone who follows you? That's up to you. I don't.

A lot of them are using software that automatically unfollows anyone who doesn't follow them back. That's not a way to build relationships. I follow people say interesting things or share posts that are really connected to my target readership.

Once you've followed some people, your "feed" will be updated quickly. Most other people will be tweeting all the time, but you don't want to see a bunch of junk. Focus more on your list of people you want to build relationships with.

Gary Vaynerchuk compares marketing to a first date: "As with any first date, getting a second date depends on you doing your best to learn more about what the other person is interested in, and directing the conversation in that direction" (*Jab, Jab, Jab, Right Hook*). Even though we're really in the *pre-marketing* stage, this advice will hold true for a while. Just because they've followed us doesn't mean they trust us, and as soon as we start blathering on about ourselves, we'll lose any chance of future interaction.

The good news is that, if you're nervous about starting out social networking because you don't know what to say, *you don't have to say very much.* You just have to listen and nod your head. When you're not famous and you don't have many followers, tweeting 100 times a day won't do much for you. What you need to do is find a way of standing out, without talking about yourself all the time.

Don't retweet—reply!

Most other people follow someone and then retweet everything they say. This kind of sucking up is marginally appreciated, but it doesn't add value or make you stand out. Successful online personalities get a lot of retweets anyway. Retweeting what they say won't impress them.

Here's what you should do instead:

1) *If they posted a link to an article, actually go and read the article. Pick out a quote or phrase from the article and send it in a new Tweet. Make sure to add their Twitter handle (using "@ theirname") in your Tweet so they'll see it.* **2)** *If they posted a statement, question, quotation, observation, etc, reply and respond to them. Don't overthink it, but don't post something lame like "great tips!" or "Wow!" Add to the conversation by commenting.* **3)** *You can also use "Quote Tweet"—rather than retweeting, it's like a retweet you can edit. Basically, instead of just retweeting the article name and link they posted, you add commentary and rephrase things so you're not just parroting them.*

Don't do it all the time, and don't do it to everything they post. That'll make you seem crazy or over-eager. Just do it to the stuff you like and actually have an opinion about. Maybe 1 in 10. You can be funny—but be careful, humor doesn't always translate, especially dark or racy humor.

If you do this for a while, the other person may check out your profile or website, and if it looks decent enough, they may actually follow you. But it doesn't matter if they don't. Because when you interact with people with a lot of followers this way, you're getting a lot of visibility.

When you create a personal and unique conversation, sometimes the other person's response to you is better than their original comment; other people will retweet THAT comment, which has your Twitter handle on it, and everybody will think "Gee, who's that important guy talking to? Maybe I should follow them too!"

Natalie Sisson, who made Forbes' list of "25 Most Influential Women Tweeting About Entrepreneurship" writes on her blog, *"I add all sorts of targets to this list, from editors I want to write for to literary agents I'm hoping will be interested in my book. Then I spend a few minutes each day browsing that list, looking for ways to subtly interact with those people—by RTing their tweets, @replying them, @mentioning them, and more. This is a big opportunity to use Twitter strategically, rather than just sort of wasting time on the network"* (Suitcaseentrepreneur.com).

When you tweet about someone else, even something simple like "Wow I just finished (this new book) by @thisauthor, it's so powerful and moving..." they'll probably reply with a "thanks" or at the very least "favorite" your tweet by tapping the star icon. But you'll pop up on the feeds of everybody who's following that person.

⭐ **Hugh Howey** favorited your Tweet   3h
3h: @hughhowey I keep telling people it's the easiest business to go into...
if you've got a story and can write.

Recently I started following Hugh Howey, and he made my week by following me back (I'm a huge fan of the *Wool* series). There's a lot of pessimism in indie publishing circles and Howey wrote about how, compared to most other "hobbies", writing was still a pretty great way to do what you love and make some money. When I replied to one of his tweets, he took a second to favorite it. About 10 people followed me immediately.

I'm not suggesting that you manipulate or use people for their influence—but you can treat them like the normal humans they are and establish a genuine relationship instead of keeping them at a distance like a rock star.

They're spending time on Twitter trying to get more followers and sharing their content, and it sucks when you post something that gets no replies, no retweets and no favorites. Be a friend and help them out, but do it by adding value, not just being robotic and liking *everything*.

(However, be cautious about what you retweet. If you keep retweeting other people's misguided promotional attempts, people will stop following you. Help them out by using smarter tweeting—we'll talk about that more when we get to Stage Three.)

What doesn't work (but seems to be the most common strategy by indie authors) is adding tons of people and then tweeting about your book all the time, or paying some service to do it for you.

What works marginally better is to retweet everybody else's posts all the time, and every once in a while (a ratio of about 1 to 100) say something about your book.

What really works is to be active, make friends, post witty comments about lots of cool things, share other people's articles and things you find interesting. The more online friends you have, the easier it will be to sell books.

What to tweet?

As I mentioned before, you don't really have to tweet much at all. Focus on interacting with others and sharing the material of the influencers you're trying to be friends with. But you also want to be seen as an authority and a contributor, so you want to post some of your own content sometimes.

Set up Google alerts for a relevant topic, something you want to be associated with (mine are for 'creativity' and 'indie authors'). Then share interesting stuff that pops up, even from smaller blogs. *Curate content.* Try to find articles that nobody else is talking about, or share it in a unique way with a comment or opinion, or by associating it with something else that's trending.

You can also share personal updates sometimes, as long as it's in line with the brand you're creating for yourself, but don't go overboard. Don't post pictures of your breakfast (unless it's *really* yummy... or your brand is about food and diet).

Using pictures, however, is an easy way to make a profoundly bigger impact. We'll talk about this more under marketing, but most people are flipping through Twitter scanning tweets, and now that you can add pictures to Twitter, you should as much as possible. Tweet something like "Snow day, curling up with a cup of hot chocolate and #shadesofgray @E_L_James" with a picture of the book and steaming mug with snow outside. Your pictures will really jump out.

Here are a few tweets that caught my eye recently:

T. W. Luedke @TWLuedke   6m
THE SHEPHERD ~ A Young Adult Paranormal Fiction Review ow.ly
/rRen9 #YA #TeenFic #ASMSG pic.twitter.com/IZSYyRW2GY

⬑ Reply ⇄ Retweet ★ Favorite ••• More

iAuthor Tom Hobbs @TheKindleWhispe   1h
How do you save a life when you have nothing to live for? Trauma
Junkie ow.ly/hnb2/ pic.twitter.com/CltRDiLe

⬑ Reply ⇄ Retweet ★ Favorite ••• More

Catherine Green @SpookyMrsGreen   37m

Alien vampires, cyberpunk-esque futures, sexual service

robots smarturl.it/GalEn pic.twitter.com/a5uyBJVNNb asmsg tjt4a...

Retweeted by Jeff Joseph Author

↩ Expand   ← Reply   ↱ Retweet   ★ Favorite   ••• More

Karynne Summars @KarynneSummars   7m

@kellyandmichael Desperate Pursuit in
Venice.Love,Passion,Obsession +Danger.
Seductive read.myBook.to/DPIV_KS pic.twitter.com/6PLEoE4Hvo

Retweeted by The Masquerade Crew

**DESPERATE
PURSUIT
IN VENICE**

KARYNNE

↩ Expand

Love Belvin @LoveBelvin
The more exposure the deeper I fell. The sex remained skilled, impassioned, combustive. amazon.com/dp/B00UPNS95M/... zEYhh pic.twitter.com/ZBcfbdBxEq

Retweeted by Finna McAndrew

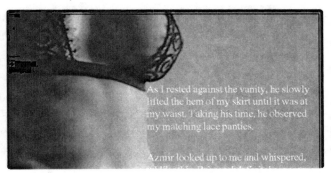

As I rested against the vanity, he slowly lifted the hem of my skirt until it was at my waist. Taking his time, he observed my matching lace panties.

Azmir looked up to me and whispered,

If these were *just text* Tweets, I would have skimmed right over them. But the pictures make you stop and look closer. The last one by Love Belvin even extends Twitter's very short character allowance and adds a racy passage, to give readers a sample. (These are examples of decent promotional tweets using images... I added them here to highlight how effective images can be; but remember not to promote or market too early or too often. This stage is really about building relationships).

If you're interested in using Pinterest as well, this is what you should be doing: 1) Find a great picture for every article your write on your blog. 2) Share the article on Twitter and Facebook, attaching the image. Also pin your image to Pinterest with a link to the blog post in the description field. Make sure the picture is related to the content, and use a few hashtags or keywords to help people find your image.

Make sure to respond to people when they retweet or favorite you. If someone talks to you ("@yourname") be friendly and helpful. Recently I told Sean Platt and Johnny B. Truant on Twitter that I liked their new book, *(Write, Publish, Repeat)* and mentioned that I would buy some of their fiction. Sean wrote back and offered to give me personal recommendations and free books—what an excellent way to make friends and build fans!

Sean Platt @SeanPlatt   14h
@Creativindie @JohnnyBTruant Thanks! I hope you love them.
Hard to pick a fav between those two, but gun to head it's The Beam
(or UW).

Sean Platt @SeanPlatt   14h
@Creativindie @JohnnyBTruant What sorts of books do you like to
read? We'll help you with the best place to start, and send you the
book.

You don't need to use hashtags as much as you think—people can still search for keywords and relevant tweets will show up whether or not you've added the "#." But you should use keywords or terms that people may search for. Hashtags can be really obnoxious. Try to make your tweets into a regular sentence. You can add a few in at the end, but don't cram them in. I also wouldn't recommend chasing hashtags (using whatever hashtags are trending).

As I'm writing this, #Christmasrocks is trending, so there are lots of strange tweets trying to use it in a sentence like "I'm making #christmasrocks cookies for #christmasrocks. Yummee! #christmasrocks." Even though nobody knows what it means, they're trying to get more visibility. But you don't need to use hashtags to get people to find you—it's far more effective to talk about them with "@theirname" or reply to their tweets with an actual conversation.

However, I should point out the article by John Kremer of *Book Marketing Bestsellers*. He sums up some recent research by TrackMaven on what makes a successful tweet. The findings show that using ALL CAPS and up to nine exclamation points (!!!!!!!!!) and over 11 hashtags will get you more retweets. I would caution that those tactics may work for the largest demographic of Twitter users, but maybe not your potential readers.

Personally, if I see an author tweet "Buy my book!" I may give it a shot, but if they used "BUY MY BOOK!!!!!!!!!" I'd block them and never give their book a chance.

The TrackMaven research compares Justin Bieber with Obama and notes that Justin is "winning" because he has a lot more retweets. But retweets don't mean sales; think about the author brand you are creating and what people will think about you. You're chasing readers, not retweeters. You want people who enjoy good writing and keep their nose in a book. If your readers are like me (sensitive introverts), having even one exclamation point can turn them off.

Also, there's a lot to be said for timing your tweets to go out during Twitter peak times. Most people tweet during office hours (daytime, Monday to Thursday), but more people use Twitter and retweet late at night or on the weekend. I live in Taiwan and don't plan so most of my tweets go out at absurd times.

How to use Facebook to make friends

First of all, using Facebook is tricky. You probably already have a normal, personal account. Should you start a page for your book? For you, the author? For a group? Making a fan page may not be successful in the beginning because nobody has heard of you or your book. A Facebook page is NOT marketing—it doesn't bring you **new** readers.

After you ask all your friends to join your fan page, you may have 13. So if you're trying to interact with anyone on Facebook, they'll think—"Damn, they only have 13 followers? They must be an amateur or someone really weird." Yes, the numbers matter. So while you can still make an author fan page and ask people to join it, it might be better to just use your normal account to get in touch with the influential people you'd like to be friends with. Plus, in my understanding of how Facebook works right now, I can add people as friends using my personal profile, but I can't do this from my fan pages—people can like *you*, but you can't friend request *them,* so using your regular personal account may be more powerful.

On the other hand, you may not want to be "friends" with a whole bunch of strangers on Facebook, so using a fan page keeps a level of professional distance. Keep in mind though that Facebook has *severely limited* fan pages: Facebook will promote your content based on whether or not it thinks people will enjoy it. I have over 600 "likes" on Facebook, but only around 10 people ever see any of my posts, which makes having a fan page pretty useless in terms of marketing.

If you want to have a fanpage but avoid the hurdle of starting with low numbers, you *can* buy followers on fiverr.com. These followers won't do anything or provide real value, but they do get the numbers up, which may help connecting with real fans in the beginning.

However, doing a big giveaway with a great prize that's attractive to your target readership and using Facebook's boosted post option will be more effective in the long run, and can also encourage people to join.

Finally, it's disadvantageous to use a pen name on Facebook, which is why I don't recommend them. You can use initials for gender neutrality, but trying to network with different names is really confusing. For connecting with professionals you really want to build relationships with, using a personal profile is probably best. The mini-celebrities you're trying to befriend may have an official page, or a group, or/and a personal page. They are probably guarded with their privacy, so sending a personal friend request may not work. You may need to join their page or group for a while and interact that way. (But don't use their pages to spam your content! What's spam? *Anything about you or your book.*)

Facebook is just like Twitter except that you can leave longer comments. And I personally prefer it to blog commenting—because they probably already have dozens of comments on their blog, and Facebook can be kind of an "afterthought" that doesn't get much attention. But this is an opportunity for you: maybe their posts get lots of shares and retweets on Twitter, but on Facebook only a handful of likes and comments. That means it's easier for you to stand out. See a post with no likes? Be the first. They'll get an instant notification that someone (you!) liked their content. Post a thoughtful reply (don't praise—interact).

You'll want to make sure you're using a universal author name and photo (I use my personal Facebook account, so my picture changes... which makes me less professional, but more personal and authentic. I can't guarantee that one works more than the other.)

When you send them a message on Facebook, they'll probably actually read it (because they get far fewer Facebook messages than email messages). But don't message them... yet. Get on their radar first by being helpful.

Facebook is a great way for people to get responses and test stuff out, so they may post questions they need answers to, or ask for feedback on some project. This is your chance to go overboard and try to help as much as you can. Find a way to make their day easier, their project more successful.

Because I was a book editor for many years, I can almost always spot typos in people's books, website articles or other content; if I see a grammar or spelling mistake I'll let them know. People joke about "grammar Nazis" but nobody wants to have typos in their content.

I also like Facebook because it's so informal. You don't get to be friends with someone just by liking their posts or helping them out. You get to be friends by sharing interests, funny moments, likes and dislikes.

Maybe you can laugh together over a funny cat video, a beautiful picture of a sunset, taunts about opposing football teams. Don't get involved in any serious, controversial topics, and don't pretend to like something if you don't, but Facebook isn't a place to focus on business. Keep it light and happy.

If you see something that you're pretty sure they'll be interested in or enjoy (and you better be *pretty sure*) you could send them a short message to tell them about it. You could also share it directly on their page but that might be spammy... if it's not your content or about you at all, it might be OK. Probably safer to send a private message and say "thought you might want to see this..."

Facebook also has groups—so you can join and interact. Remember, we're not promoting our books yet, we're adding value and building relationships. So you can share, and comment and like, and you can talk about personal stuff like your opinions, but don't *try to make anybody do anything* (like go buy your book or join your fan page).

One more thing I love about Facebook—when it's someone's birthday Facebook recommends sending them a gift. I've been passing out $25 Starbucks coupons to a lot of my friends and connections (I got this tip from the brilliant Peter Shankman). $25 isn't much, but it feels like a pretty big deal because so few people actually do it. Sending out a coupon to a *total stranger* will seem weird, so make sure you've had a few casual chats and they know who you are first.

How to use LinkedIn to make friends

After reading *How to Sell More Books Using LinkedIn* by Victoria Ipri and Austin Briggs. I knew I could be using LinkedIn more effectively in my book marketing. So I spent a four-hour bus ride (from Tainan to Taipei) checking it out and updating my profile. Now I'm hooked.

Twitter is about sharing bits of news or thoughts or information *very quickly* to lots of people.

Facebook is about interacting with your friends casually and being entertained.

Only **LinkedIn** is actually meant for building professional relationships.

So while on Facebook, going through your friends' friend list looking for people to add may be a little creepy, on LinkedIn it's just smart use of the platform.

On Twitter people are oversensitive about who's following them (if you unfollow me, I'll unfollow you!). On Facebook, getting a friend request from a stranger may seem unnerving. "Who *is* that guy?" (Especially because, until you're friends, you probably can't see much about each other.)

But LinkedIn encourages connections. So it's fine to search for people and add them. You can find one influencer, click on their profile, then "Connections" and see all the people they're connected to. Then you can connect with anyone you want.

However... a mistake I made for a while was pressing the big blue "Send Invitation" button which actually sends out the message:

> ### I'd like to add you to my professional network.
> ### —Derek Murphy

That just shows you're lazy. They might accept anyway, but you'll be very forgettable. So I changed mine to,

> ### Just making friends on LinkedIn, you seem
> ### like you're doing awesome things.
> ### —Derek Murphy

Which is OK for strangers... but if it's someone on your list, you should really know a lot about them, so make it personal. If they're friends with someone you're friends with (really friends, not strangers who follow each other) mention it. On the other hand, you don't want to seem like a stalker or a raving fanatic, so be casual, and brief.

Another reason I like LinkedIn is that it adds another layer to your relationship with people. Maybe you've been talking about them on Facebook or Twitter and sharing their content. Then when you show up on LinkedIn they'll recognize you. You can say, "Hey I really love what you do, I just wanted to connect with you on LinkedIn so I don't miss anything." How can they say no to someone that's interested in their articles and posts? It's another reminder that you're out there and that you're a person who appreciates and supports them.

LinkedIn also has groups and discussions, which can be good ways to interact. Focus on providing help and advice. Try not to disagree or argue, those threads can get heated and carried away.

Making yourself look amazing in 3 words

I know we talked earlier about the importance of your "author story," but even more so than Twitter, your picture and very short self-description are crucial on LinkedIn. On Twitter people will become aware of you through your interaction or what you say and share. LinkedIn users are more discerning: they are looking for *business contacts* that will be mutually beneficial, which means they're scrolling through hundreds of accounts (and on a smartphone they can only see about half of your already short bio). You need to convince them, *in just a couple words* that you are worth knowing.

Here are a few mistakes to avoid:

- Don't waste space with meaningless words like "Professional"
- Don't use long words like "communications, entrepreneur, marketing..."
- "CEO, CO-Founder, Partner" sounds less impressive when you've already seen hundreds of others—especially if the company name or website is cut off.
- Try not to divide between roles. If you HAVE to, use commas, not forward slashes. ("Author, blogger and entrepreneur"—not "author/blogger/entrepreneur." But those are both pretty weak.)
- What makes you different and special? What benefits do you provide? Can you sum it up into a catchprase or tagline? Can you subtitle yourself?

Instead of "Fantasy writer of *This Novel*" how about "Magical landscapes to get lost in." Instead of "I write thrillers" how about "Writing that makes you clench your teeth and grip the sheets."

Using your website

Throughout this stage, even though you're not promoting anything or talking about your book, you'll still be *soft-selling*. In your profile, you probably have "author of *ThisBook*" or at least a link to your website. As people become aware of you, and start liking you more and more because you're so helpful and charming and friendly, they'll find out more about you and check out your book. *They won't do it* if you ask them to, so you must resist the urge. But you still want to have everything set up so that if, on their own initiative, they check you out, your material is strong enough to make the sale (and it should be, because we focused on that part in Stage One).

So let's say you have your amazing blog set up. You've joined LinkedIn, Twitter and Facebook. You have your social media profile links on your blog, as well as your "Buy Now/Read a Sample" links. What else can you do to start getting more interaction?

In John Locke's book *How I Sold 1 Million eBooks in 5 Months!* he describes a process that goes something like this:

- Identify fans of something you are also a fan of, and search for hashtags of that topic.
- Write a glowing, warm article of praise about that topic on your blog and invite Twitter users who are writing about that topic to view your article.

- Those fans will share your article, because they love the topic.
- Lots of people will visit your website, where you have your books listed for sale on the sidebar.

The basic idea is that people will automatically like you when you agree with them about something they are passionate about, and they will buy your books because you've made them feel good about themselves. (I can hear my own cynicism in that sentence, but it's not much different than the approach in Dale Carnegie's *Make Friends and Influence People*.) There's no question that the strategy works, so you may want to <u>grab Locke's book on Amazon</u>.

Austin Kleon shares a similar strategy in *Steal Like an Artist*:

> "*I recommend public fan letters. The Internet is really good for this. Write a blog post about someone's work that you admire and link to their site. Make something and dedicate it to your hero. Answer a question they've asked, solve a problem for them, or improve on their work and share it online.*"

A lot of people use Google Alerts for their own name so they can track what people are saying about them, but you could also link to your post on Twitter and

"@" them. They may read your post and like it. Even if they don't, other people who like that person will find it. More people will find a post written about someone famous than a general post not talking about anybody specifically.

You can also get a lot of traffic with "linkbait" articles. For example, you could write about the "Top 25 indie authors you need to follow" with a short description of each, their Twitter handles and a link to their book. Several if not most of them will link back and share your article.

Yet another reminder: You may be brilliant at Facebook, LinkedIn and Twitter, but you'll get nowhere with an ugly website. Less is more. Take off all the pretty pictures and bold colors and scroll-flourishes and fancy fonts. Take off anything that moves or beeps or flashes or slides. Make sure it's dead-easy to share your posts, your writing, your pictures, or go buy your book. If it isn't... take your website out of your marketing strategy.

Note: I considered adding Reddit to this section. Reddit users are active and passionate and tech-savvy; if you create an account, you can join various 'sub-reddits' or groups, and submit links. Although Reddit hates spammers and promoting your own links is frowned upon, there are a few areas dedicated to indie authors or book promotion. But like all other platforms, Reddit will only work if you put in the time to comment and interact, share useful content, and help others to build relationships before trying to market your book.

MARKETING

You may think it's silly for a book marketing guide to avoid talking about actually marketing your book until 2/3 of the way in, but marketing of any kind would fail dismally without having a solid platform (nice cover, sales copy, reviews and functional website), and even then it's unlikely to be successful without having online relationships (for social proof and to reach more people). Too many people (even book marketing gurus and book marketing *companies*) go straight for the bullhorn.

That's why you see stuff like this everywhere:

"Great new book #bestselling #award winning #selfpub five star review says, "You can't miss this!!!" on sale TODAY ONLY, get it HERE!!!"

Jeff Goins wrote a post recently called "Don't Promote," where he says "Self-promotion is a misnomer. You don't promote yourself; others do that for you. Otherwise, you're just patting yourself on the back. All great promotion comes from other people. Nobody wants to listen to a self-promoter."

What this means: you're allowed to *share your content,* but you can't promote it. What's the difference?

This is a share: "Hey, my new book is out, if you have a minute could you help me share it?"

This is promotion: "Life-changing book, sexy and wicked, get it here for half off!!!"

It's true, if you don't have any friends, that the "promotion" may drive more sales than the weaker and more casual "share." And actually the one I wrote above isn't *that* bad. But you don't want to use it a whole bunch of times, for weeks and weeks, because it will quickly lose its power. This is especially true because so many authors are using very similar self-promotion strategies. In a Copyblogger article by Amy Harrison called "3 Ways the Magic of Dr. Seuss can help you create unforgettable copy", Amy introduces the "Broca" part of our brain:

> "Basically, as we become more familiar with language, our Broca area skips over what feels predictable. So if we see the same words, phrases, and clichés, they simply don't have the

same impact as when we read them the first time around. In his book The Magical Worlds of the Wizard of Ads, Roy H. Williams states that for adverts to cut through the noise they need to be different enough to wake up the Broca area ... but not so different that the audience discards the idea outright. In other words, your audience has to feel your content is new, but also credible."

So here are two things to keep in mind:

- EVEN though now you've got some friends and credibility and social karma, you'll lose it as soon as you start spamming about your book.
- Whatever your message, it has to be new and different, it has to stand out.

Now that we're actually going to start marketing, we'll take a look the *best marketing strategies* to help you sell books. I'll show you some examples of how to use Twitter, Facebook and a few other sites, plus leverage the relationships you've been making.

Guest Posting

To make your book succeed you need to get it in front of the people who would enjoy reading it. If you are writing Mysteries, look for organizations, websites or blogs aimed at readers or authors of that genre.

If you've narrowed down your space, and found a few perfect blogs or websites, then you have two options.

You can contact them about advertising and pay a fee to put up an ad on their site, or you can make friends with the owner by offering to share some custom written guest posts.

Asking another blog or website to talk about your book is probably doomed to failure. Nobody else cares about you or your book enough to help you promote it, especially if you're a complete stranger asking them to write an article for you.

NEVER ASK FOR FAVORS. Either pay for advertising, or offer a custom guest post that is beneficial to the blog owners. You will set yourself apart from the thousands of other indie authors mass-emailing "please help me out" letters.

As Seth Godin writes in his post 8 Email Failures, "The thing you need me to do better be fun, worth doing and generous. If it's not, I'm not going to do it, no matter how much you need me to do it."

How to write a guest post. Most blogs make money depending on how many "hits" or "visits" they get. So if you want to write a guest post, you need to write an article that solves a problem a lot of people are trying to solve, or offers information about something a lot of people want to learn about, and the article should also fit the blog you're targeting. So you have to do a little research, read previous articles on that blog, find something you have an opinion and some knowledge about, and write the article.

You could "pitch" a few ideas, but not everybody will write you back, whereas if you had a finished article and the blogger can just copy, paste and post it, you'd be saving them some time and they wouldn't have to take a risk on you finishing a decent article.

If I *really wanted* a guest post on a specific site, I would write three different articles. You'll need to spend some time researching how to write article headers for blogs (catchy and full of keywords). Copyblogger.com is a great resource for getting started. After each article write a short Bio, "*Pete Thompson has been a defense lawyer for 20 years. His new novel "The Lawyer's Kiss" is a thrilling look at the dark world of corporate sexual misconduct.*" (I just made all that up, but you get the point.)

This will only work if the article *and* your book will appeal to readers who visit that site, and if it brings traffic to the blogger. If he posts one, maybe he'll post the other two later (make sure to let him know that's OK, or whether you plan to use those articles somewhere else). Either way, you've given him some free content he can use to build up his blog, and that's good for him. He's not doing you any favors. You're building an equal-value relationship. (Although this will be much easier if you've already interacted with the blogger on social media and they know who you are.)

When writing to a blogger, follow these rules:

- Keep it really short (a couple sentences).
- Focus on a way to pitch that provides value for *them* and their readers, not you.

Example pitch: *Hi (name), I'm looking for a way to boost my visibility and wanted to offer you a few guest posts I think your readers will like. Here are three titles I've come up with, the articles are finished and I've attached them here. You can find out more about me and what I'm doing on my website, www.mywebsite.com. Let me know if you have any questions. I've been reading your blog for a while and some of your articles (like "this title" and "this title" have really inspired/motivated me).*

PS) A simple trick for pitching anything: don't compliment at the beginning of your email. Ask for what you want first, then compliment at the end. People are far more likely to believe the compliments and praise this way, which will improve your success rate.

Guest posting can be a powerful way to promote books. This is what Tim Ferriss has used repeatedly to keep his books at the top of the best-seller lists for years. In fact he was one of the first to do it really well, and as someone who does everything over the top, he actually attended big blogging conferences, went up and introduced himself to top bloggers and asked them out for drinks or coffee so he could pitch his book. But still, when he's promoting a new book, Tim doesn't call in any favors. He crafts a very careful, well written guest article on a topic of interest to the blog he's pitching. Another writer who's been prodigious at using guest posts to build a platform is Jeff Goins. If you get a chance to join his _Tribe Writers class_, you should.

Press Releases (usually don't work)

It doesn't matter how catchy and well-written they are, a press release about a book usually won't do much. Which is why the "press release" services of author marketing companies probably aren't worth buying.

Even if they help you write it.

Even if you have a big sale or promotion or are giving money away to charity.

EVEN if you have an amazing book.

Why? Because publishing a book isn't a story.

Blogs, newspapers, TV reporters, they want to share a story that's interesting, unique, thought-provoking, novel, fun. They want something that makes you go "Oh!" A press release about a book is boring. ANY book.

It goes like this:

_____

FOR IMMEDIATE RELEASE

Date | Location

Today some brilliant author, winner of a bunch of cool awards, published the first and only book—sure to change your life, and the whole world—that accurately portrays the relationship between microbacterial intestinal fauna and psychological health through a charming analogy about a boy and his pet turtle. "Lessons I learned from Pete" is 250,000 words long and illustrated by woodcut etchings from Singapore's premiere artist, Xian Shir Tan.

The book will be available on Christmas Day 2013 to the delight of children everywhere so make sure you get it under your tree in time! 1/2 of all proceeds will go to support 1 legged drug addict elephants in China, and there will be a 75% off discount to the first 1000 buyers.

For more information and a full press kit, go to theauthorswebsite.com

---

Even if you make a press release super interesting—it's still boring. News stories are things that happen. You publishing a book is not news. You need to DO SOMETHING that makes you newsworthy.

A book by itself is an inanimate object. If readers love it they will share it, so you need to get it in front of them and remove all obstacles to purchasing. But you can't promote it with a press release.

You can promote yourself, or a project/activity you've created or are involved in, if it's interesting. If it's a non-fiction book there's probably a bigger backstory about what you actually do, but for a fiction that backstory may be "spent 300 hours up too late drinking coffee and being antisocial..."

You can use a press release to promote your book *indirectly*. To do this, you need to think bigger, involve more people, make a bigger impact, and think about what event you can plan or organize that will be interesting enough to be real news. You need to make something that has meaning, that makes people feel something emotionally, that taps into a movement, an opinion or a crisis.

For example:

Yesterday, a group of 500 self-publishing authors banded together in an effort to support 1 legged drug addict elephants in China. These authors have all been able to make a living through writing and are now beginning to put their success to good use. This project is another indicator that self-publishing has become mainstream and is a respectable publishing model. The project is being organized by Author Name, whose book "Lessons I learned from Pete" has been on the bestseller lists for 15 weeks. For a full list of the 500 authors, <u>click here.</u>

This isn't the best example, but you get the point. People will share the story, because the story is interesting. You and your book—you're the footnote, not the main event.

In Trust Me I'm Lying Ryan Holiday talks about Tucker Max's book (*Assholes Finish First*, I believe). They put up a huge billboard and arranged to have a few protesters spray paint over it with feminine power stuff. The story of a guy writing a book about being an asshole isn't a story. But the story of some women responding to the misogynist, male-centric book with vandalism creates a real story—a viral story, of controversy—which was picked up again and again by huge media and TV broadcasts. (It doesn't have to be a real story—it can be a really good idea of a *potential story*).

Press releases don't really matter, because they aren't how the news works anymore. The blog posts I write are just about as likely to get picked up by Google News as your Press Release. If a lot of people share it, then it would become the source for bigger blogs. If it got enough shares and likes and comments, eventually the TV news would pick it up. In *Author 101*, Rick Frishman says:

> "To attract press, you need headlines about Money, Sex, Health, Controversy. You need bold, daring, risqué headers. Take chances; be provocative, naughty and controversial."

For a non-fiction, your press release should 'solve' not sell. List a problem that you or your book solves and actually SOLVE it, don't hint, give real actionable advice to prove your book's value.

If you have a very specific book aimed at a very specific, organized group ("Gardening for Vietnam vets with PTSD") then a press release might get the attention of people who are on the lookout for specific terms, and they may share your news.

Otherwise, you need to create a story around yourself by turning your book into an event. No, not like a book launch party or book signing. Think bigger! How about organizing an Indie Author Association for your city and throwing an extravagant "dress up like your main character" party? That would be news!

Let's say you wrote a post-apocalyptic novel. Here's what I would do:

- Go on ebay and buy a bunch of gas masks and old goggles. They have some excellent steampunk stuff on there.
- Go on Craigslist and hire 20 guys to dress up and walk around town for a couple hours (or better yet, appear at some big event that's already going to be covered).
- Get video and pictures, write an article, publish it as a press release and also as an article on a couple of tiny blogs.

- Email a few bigger blogs and say "Hey did you guys hear about this? Crazy" and hope they share the story.

It doesn't matter, in the beginning, that anybody who actually saw those guys in gas masks knew about you or your book. I wouldn't have them handing out postcards or flyers. Just walking around town like no big deal. Other people will see them, and maybe freak out a little, especially when they see more than one. They'll probably call the police, or go search online, and everybody will want to know WHY and WHAT happened. It'll be a mystery. Then later, it'll become a story. They'll get eye-witnesses. And it will be revealed it was all a publicity stunt for a new book. Did you see the <u>coffee shop publicity stunt</u> they pulled for the *Carrie* movie? That's the kind of thing that people share.

Granted, a publicity stunt of this size is risky, and you better have a damn fine book. If you invite hundreds of thousands of people to suddenly look for you and your book, your website better be polished, your author photos better be professional, and your book better be good.

I don't think it matters so much anymore if its indie published, as long as it's clean, formatted, stylish, well designed, and a good story (I also don't think the writing matters as much. A good story trumps all).

I will pause for a moment to beleaguer this point: book promotion and marketing *may not even be good* for your book. Visibility will only help a book succeed **or fail** faster. And if you get publicity while your book is underdressed, underpolished, and has zero reviews, or has boring description text, you will have made a bad first impression and all other attempts will be dismissed.

Don't cry wolf. Don't go out in public naked. Protect your self-published book from instant rejection by surrounding it with a professional appearance. But if your book is *already* selling, and most people seem to like it, by all means get it in front of more people to speed up its obvious trajectory.

A press release can also be a good way to get a lot of "backlinks" that make your blog more trustworthy, so you can consider it as a way to boost your page rank... and you will probably get some random traffic and might see a bump in sales (but again, this depends a lot on whether there are keywords people are on the lookout for). Most book press releases disappear into the interwebs. I'm not saying "don't do it", but don't make it your main strategy, and don't spend too much, and make it an awesome story that people will want to share.)

If you can't think of any news besides "hey I wrote a book!" then you're better off paying for book advertising than wasting money on a press release.

How to market without promoting your book

You can use the bullhorn effect and just yell at everybody really loudly, but it will backfire if you're too annoying. The new marketing—which is far too scarce among authors—is to create positive relationships by providing value: it's not about selling, it's about sharing things that other people will enjoy, helping them solve their problems, caring about them, and making things easier for them.

99% of authors don't want to do any of that stuff. They just want people to buy their book. **But that's why it will work for you.** If you have a blog or social media profiles, less than 10% should be directly about your own book, which means you've got to find 90% worth of other stuff to talk about!

If you're promoting on social media, you need to use what Gary Vaynerchuk calls "native content" in his book *Jab, Jab, Jab Right Hook*. This means your posts should look, sound and feel the same as all the other stuff on that platform. They need to provide "The same value and emotional benefits people are seeking when they come to the platform in the first place; it's whatever hits your emotional center so hard you have to share it with someone else. When native content is skillfully delivered, a person will consume it with the same interest as he would anyone else's. That's because unlike most of the marketing tactics forced down consumer's throats in the past, smart, native social media should **enhance the consumer's interaction with the platform, not distract him from it."** He continues,

> "Make it simple. Make it memorable. Make it inviting to look at. Make it fun to read. Make it for your customer or your audience, not for yourself. Because when you jab, you're not selling anything. You're not asking your consumer for a commitment. You're just sharing a moment together. Something funny, ridiculous, clever, dramatic, informative or heartwarming."

Think about the types of readers who will enjoy your book. What are their fears, wishes, hobbies, pastimes, dreams? What is their location, age group, race? Where do they hang out? How do they spend their time online? The more detailed answers you can provide, the better you'll be able to figure out how to reach them—either by advertising where they are, or creating something fun, meaningful and interesting that they can enjoy.

It doesn't have to be related to your book, at all. A brilliant example of smart marketing I saw recently was Lydia Kang's buzzfeed "<u>Weird things that authors do</u>." It's a very simple list, illustrated with short videos, which is cute and funny and easily shareable. It doesn't have anything directly to do with her novel, *Control*, but it's becoming viral and getting a lot of traffic. At the bottom of the post is a short by-line about the author.

There's no hard sell, or buy link, or special discount to buy the book right now. Nothing. Just cool, free content she made, that authors will like and share. That's the kind of content you should be creating: things that are valuable that aren't about your book, that you can post on bigger blogs with more traffic.

Your book is not news. Your book is not viral content. You need to do *other things*, that aren't your book, to get some attention so that you can very quietly and subtly show off your book. And if it's great and people love it, it will be successful.

Paid Advertising

To market your book on social media, you need to make fun stuff that doesn't distract from the platform. If you can't do that, focus on advertising. People probably aren't on Twitter or Facebook looking for book recommendations. Go to Goodreads or other review sites where people are actually looking for something to read. Those are great places to pay for ads which lead people back to your book.

Don't be one of those authors who are buying advertising with money that would be better spent on a new book cover, an editor for their sales copy, a nicer website or some reviews.

But if your platform is strong and you've tested it and know that it can convert browsers into buyers, paying for more traffic may be worth it. You can start on Facebook or Project Wonderful. Hire someone to make amazing banner ads, or use this http://www.bannersnack.com to make something really cool (better yet, don't: hire someone on fiverr.com to make you nice ads). Spend $20. See if you make enough sales to earn your money back.

If not, get a stranger (on fiverr.com?) to give you feedback on your sales copy and cover. Tweak everything. Make it stronger. Make sure you have at least 10 reviews. Then do it again.

On Project Wonderful you'll be able to test different things like advertising on different blogs, and you pay per day rather than per click, and it's very cheap.

First of all you need to figure out how many views or impressions it takes to get how many clicks. Facebook will also give you these details. And you can choose viewers by what they like - so for Facebook ads, target viewers who have "liked" books you think yours compares to. If I wrote a legal thriller, I would want my ad to show up for people who liked "The Firm."

You should also use "Facebook Graph Searches." Jon Loomer points out on this page how you can just type into the search box on Facebook "Pages liked by people who liked..." So I could start by trying to understand my own fans and use "Pages liked by people who liked Creativindie" (?)

But it's not all about clicks: you also need to figure out if the people clicking are buying anything. There are fancy tools to do this but I'm lazy, so I would just estimate. Say I usually sell 1 book a day: that's my baseline. Then I run Facebook ads and sell 4 books a day. If 100 people clicked my ad today, and I sold 3 extra books, that means for every 33 (approx.) people who click my ad, I only get 1 sale. That's not too bad, but not great.

Maybe my ad is awesome, and 1000 people clicked—but I still only got 3 extra sales... then I would be in trouble—especially if I'm paying per click.

So you don't want your ad to appeal to everyone. You want to get rid of everybody who's not a serious buyer. You do that by providing enough information. Be clear about the book, the genre, the setting, the main conflict (hint, don't actually give it away). You need to hook only the kind of people who are really going to love your book, and not a bunch of people who won't. You want less clicks, but more conversions.

If you are converting 1 in 30, you could probably improve your Amazon or sales page. Even if your book is not great—they don't know that yet. If you have a great sales description, a great cover and at least 10 reviews, you should be able to close 1 in 10 visitors who clicked on your ad.

This is why you don't want to advertise your book on just any blog's sidebar—you're paying to show that ad to everybody. I just visited a mediocre, PR2 blog about books that allows advertising for $150 a week. They already have 6 books in their sidebar, which means they're making $3600 a month doing nothing but cashing in on the desperation of indie authors! It's true they might get a lot of traffic (doubtful, I also caught some spelling errors in their own banner ads...) but the people visiting a book marketing blog are *probably not* your target readers. It would be much more effective to figure out who your readers are and where they are, than to just advertise wherever you can.

You can do this with Google Adwords: figure out the keywords that your readers search for when they want to find a new book. Maybe they type "paranormal romance" or "books like Twilight" or "dark teen fiction." Figure out what they search for and find a keyword with a lot of searches but not much competition. Then write a Google ad saying something that appeals specifically to those readers. For example, "Miss Bella and Edward? Yearning for some more Supernatural Love? Click here" (that's too long for Google but you get the point).

Don't know what kind of reader you're looking for? Answer these questions by filling in the blanks.

- People who liked __famous book__ will like my book.
- People who are interested in these topics will like my book.
- People who have had this experience will like my book.
- People from this social background who are about this age will like my book.

Got it? Now that you know something about your ideal readers, you need to find them. Look for organizations, blogs, websites or other online places that your perfect reader likes to visit.

Let's say that you are writing a historical romance. What if you made a Facebook page called "I LOVE HISTORICAL ROMANCE" or something like that. You will be inviting exactly the kind of people who might like your book. They will join the page, not to support you, but to tell the world something about *themselves*. And of course, as the administrator of the Fanpage, you can add in info about your book from time to time.

The lesson: Don't make it about you or your book. Create the type of space your key readers would like to be found in, or the type of group key readers would join. Or, seek out the groups that already exist and tell them about your book.

Posting comments about your book will probably be seen as spam, so find a way to advertise. Write an ad that is about your readers and identifies what they want. This will work better than the far more common:

Great book! This reviewer says, "Awesome!" On sale today!

Readers don't care about reviews until after they are interested—you need to interest them first by targeting and fulfilling their needs.

Google Adwords is also pretty great because you can target specific blogs. If you look on Blogads, for example, savvy blogs are already charging a few hundred bucks for a week of advertising.

And if you contact a specific blog directly, they may quote you as much. But a lot of the same blogs use a combination of advertising, including Google Adwords; and you can set up a network of blogs and have your ads show only on those sites.

You can also go to "Tools and Analysis" and "Display Planner" to get ideas of where to advertise. For example, type in the keyword "Technothriller" to find some sites you can advertise on; click "individual targeting ideas" then "placements." I was looking for something like "Thrillerbooks.com", unfortunately all I found were a bunch of much bigger book websites.

Sure you could advertise on Goodreads or LibraryThing to try it out, but it isn't very targeted. Big traffic sites cost more to advertise, so you spend more, but your ad is showing to a lot of people who aren't looking for a thriller. Still, if you're paying for clicks and your ad says "Technothriller" then you'll only pay for the Technothriller fans who click the ad.

Try it and see if it's worth the money.

What you want to find are small sites with less traffic, but very primed (ready to buy) traffic. People get more specific with their search terms as they get closer to purchase. For example if I'm buying a laptop, I'll search for "Best laptops 2013" and then "17inch I-7 Acer notebook" as I figure out what I want.

So you could use Google adwords to buy very cheap ads on some small sites with less traffic, but experience much better results (I like Project Wonderful for this—lots of little but specific sites, so they charge next to nothing).

When I searched Google for "Technothriller," the first 3 or 4 pages were just big websites, but there was a Yahoo Answers with a question like "What are the best 10 thrillers you've ever read?" Since it came up early in search results, that page is going to get a lot of traffic. And Yahoo answers is free—you can login (better to have a friend do it) and say "hey I just read this book (your title here) and it was great, check it out." Boom, free advertising.

Otherwise make a note of mid-sized blogs with good traffic but that aren't real slick or business-oriented. If they're running Google ads, you can advertise on their site—often for much less than it would cost to advertise directly with them. If they aren't running ads, but think they have the right kind of traffic, send them an email with an offer ($50 a month is reasonable for small to mid-sized blogs).

Final points

1. Don't use a shotgun approach and pay to advertise your book everywhere. Make sure you're advertising to readers who will be interested. Make sure you screen them by using a detailed ad that only appeals to readers very likely to buy.

2. Don't spend very much. Spend $20, then tweak, then another $20. Make sure the people who click the ad actually buy the book—or at least a lot of them. Tighten things up, see if you can get it down to 1 in 10.

3. Your book cover, sales copy (book summary) and sales page (your own site or Amazon) are probably not good enough. You need at least 10 reviews. If you're trying to advertise with a mediocre book cover, average ho-hum sales description and a handful of reviews, you're almost certainly throwing money away.

4. IF you figure out how to advertise so that you're making money—as in, for every $20 you spend, you sell 20 books (and make $40) then brilliant—go all in. Spend $200 and see if you can make $400. But keep in mind at some point you will saturate your targets. After everybody who's seen your ad has bought the book, they aren't going to buy it again. So, if you keep advertising in the same places, eventually your results will drop.

Facebook Sponsored Posts

Facebook sponsored posts can be very powerful if used well. IF you see something you posted on Facebook get better than average interaction (people seem to be liking, commenting and sharing—THEN you should pay for a sponsored ad to help it reach more people. Facebook wants to show people stuff they like, so if it's getting a good response, their algorithms will automatically start promoting your post naturally and stop charging you for it. It isn't quite like advertising, so advertising a book won't work so well. You need to create some "native content" that people really love. It can make a giveaway or contest much more effective.

On one of my Facebook groups recently, I posted a contest to win a funny ugly Christmas sweater. Only about a dozen people saw my post naturally, so I spent $100 to boost the post. It reached 47,000 people and got about 50 comments. I also added a few hundred people to my Facebook group. The trick is to A) provide something new and cool that they want B) make it very easy for them to take action.

I tried to duplicate my success with a promotion for this book, but failed. I'm sharing the data below.

		267 Total Engagements	$0.11 Per Post Engagement	2,479	12/20/2013 11:59AM	12/21/2013 8:59AM	$40.00
Post: "Win a one-week writer's vacation and finish that..."		44 Total Engagements	$0.91 Per Post Engagement	12,317	12/20/2013	12/21/2013 8:59AM	$40.00
Post: "To promote my new book marketing guide, I'm..."		200 Total Engagements	$0.50 Per Post Engagement	73,250	12/20/2013	12/21/2013 8:59AM	$100.00

First I spent $100 with a soft-sell, "to promote my new book..." it got 200 post engagements (likes, comments or shares) so it ended up costing .50 per engagement. Although it got a lot of views, there was very little interaction and I don't think it sold many books (even though the book was free, and the prize was a one week resort vacation.) Since I wasn't getting much reaction, I tried a similar post that focused on the benefits "Win a one-week writer's vacation and finish that book in 2014!" It got *even less* engagment... but maybe because many people had already seen the first post. I also think it is too promotional - it seems like an ad or gimmick. It might get some interest but it doesn't impress, surprise or create an emotional response. But I still wanted to do some promotion, so I decided to focus on something else I thought people might like and share, my DIY book covers. I made a new post called "Can you believe these book covers were made in MS Word?" I was hoping to get more likes for my page, and hopefully people would also see the two earlier posts. Although it got a lot of engagement, in the end I only added about 10 new followers.

Lessons learned: Facebook sponsored posts can help you share your best content to new viewers, but there needs to be an extremely simple call to action ("like this page" or "just comment below") and the content should be something fun, interesting, but non-promotional.

When to pay for book marketing

I'm a casual browser of book marketing and promotion sites. I also deal with a lot of authors asking about book promotion companies and services. In general, I say to steer clear. Paying someone else to market your book is a losing gamble, and you'll very rarely make even a fraction of your money back. As they say on their websites, they can't guarantee sales. Which means, they get paid regardless of whether you sell more books. So they may not take the time to write the best press release, craft the best sales pitch, or write the best Amazon summary.

Spending thousands of dollars on book publicity may seem like a bold, powerful play—a professional move that shows you're serious—but you should try other things before getting out your checkbook.

More importantly, book publicity can be a waste because you are giving up control. When you pay someone else to promote or publicize your book, you are giving up power. You are trading their time and effort for potential book sales, but after they've stopped working for you (once the money's gone) you're no better off than you were before.

That means that whenever you want to sell more books, you've got to spend more money on advertising and publicity.

There is nothing that book promoters are doing that you couldn't do yourself. They'll help find and tell your story, help craft your press release and submit it to news agencies, send out hundreds of emails to reporters trying to get a review or story, call radio shows. You're paying for their time and expertise, and some of it can pay off (it saves you a lot of time, and if your time is very valuable— more valuable than theirs—then go ahead).

Here's an easy way to tell if they secretly think you're an easy mark—they let you pay them to market a book with an ugly cover, no reviews and poor sales copy on the Amazon page. They know that no matter what they do, it's all in vain, and nobody's going to buy your book anyway. But they'll still go through the motions because hey, you paid for it.

If you are going to pay for book publicity or marketing, make sure...

1) The cover is brilliant—don't spend money to market an ugly book.

2) The story is good (verified by positive, unbiased reviews).
3) Your author website is awesome; the book summary is well-crafted.

A professional book publicist can help you tell your story and connect it with larger issues that are relevant to current events (without this, no press is going to cover your book), and I'm willing to say *if the book has a lot of potential* a publicist may be the solution to truly break out and become a bestseller. The problem is that many publicists are getting paid to publicize a product with no chance of success, and they probably know it.

In general, I think making online relationships and paying for advertising will be a lot more cost effective than hiring a book publicist; even if your time is very valuable and you want someone else to do everything for you, you could hire a virtual assistant to do manual tasks for you without coming close to the price most book publicists charge.

And, there's a good chance that publicity isn't your problem at all... you may have a product problem, so make sure all of your basics are perfect first, test out your conversion with advertising, make sure your book is finding the right target readers and that feedback is positive. If not, hiring a publicist won't help, because *they can't fix the product*. (Actually I've started to notice some book marketing packages that include a cover design makeover, which is smart.) If you're thinking about paying a lot of money for marketing, join Author Marketing Club first. The annual fee is not much and there are some really powerful tools you can use to sell more books.

Pricing Strategies

Something I haven't brought up yet, but is crucial to sales (especially in the beginning) is pricing. I see a lot of authors trying to sell, market or advertise books that are priced high—in the $5 to $10 range (for the Kindle version). Remember that you're not competing against mainstream books, you're competing against all other indie authors as well, and low pricing is an effective marketing strategy. Mark Coker of Smashwords recently published a large study on pricing and found $3.99 to be the optimal pricing point for sales and earnings. The important thing to remember in the very beginning is that it's not about the sales, it's about generating fans, comments and reviews that will drive sales. For that reason, launching your book (after everything is polished, tested and perfect) with a free giveaway is the best way to get started.

KDP select and more

So what if you've got a great book for sale? Most people buy their books at the bookstore, or they check out the best-seller lists. Why should they buy your book? If your sales copy and reviews and sales page is all amazingly compelling and creates a burning desire to read the book, you'll probably get some sales... but especially when you're starting out, you need to sweeten the deal.

If you opt into Amazon's Kindle Select Program, for example, you can list your book for 5 free days. During those 5 days, you can promote your book to dozens of popular websites that tell readers about free Kindle books; it's also much easier to ask your friends and followers to download it and post a review—because *it'll be free for the next 5* days. (It creates a sense of urgency, and removes the price barrier.) I've heard authors tell me over and over again, they get *tens of thousands of downloads* during this period. Those downloads result in reviews, and more sales down the road.

A generous resource list of websites that will promote your free Kindle book can be found in the back of Cheryl Kaye Tardif's "How I Made Over $42,000 in 1 Month Selling My Kindle eBooks." There's also a tool in Author Marketing Club that submits your free book to a bunch of sites automatically.

If you have a print version, you can do a giveaway on GoodReads. If you're focusing on reviews, you can offer a big prize for the "most helpful" review on Amazon and time it with your free days (so there is no barrier to entry).

FREE is a valuable tool for removing resistance. If you write serials (if you don't, you should) or even if you write non-fiction, think about how you can write a shorter version of your book, or short story, or add-on article, that you can give away for free. Then you can keep your main book up a little higher. I recommend free or .99cents to start with for any book, until you are making consistent sales and getting lots of positive reviews. If your book is good and you take away buyer resistance, you'll get reviews. Later, you can bump the price up, but almost all of the indie authors who are making millions or getting publishing deals sold their books at very, very low prices. It works.

You can also encourage sales and downloads by offering something extra, something of inherent value. For example, you could offer on your website, "Anybody who buys the book and posts a review on Amazon will get a $15 Starbucks Card—first 10 reviews only." Sure, you're buying reviews. But you may have a surge of sales (maybe a hundred if you're lucky?) and you only have to buy 10 cards (that's $150, plus shipping... or you can send online coupons). Not too bad an investment if it boosts your sales and reviews.

PS) I screwed up my KDP select free days by using them just before Christmas. I miscalculated how much Christmas disrupts ebook sales - while the season is great for gifting, it's not so great for buying books, and people are too busy to relax and curl up with a good read. Once I realized this - as well as the fact that tens of thousands of people would be getting Kindles and tablets for Christmas and downloading free books, I paused my campaign and set it to finish up on Dec. 25th and 26th. Also, because this is a non-fiction book for writers hoping to sell more books, the peak opportunity would have been just before and after New Year's, when people are in the goal-planning and making resolutions stage.

The book launch

The point of a book launch is to offer a lot of big, tangible benefits and rewards all at once, to get the ball rolling. The best book launch I've seen recently was for Jeff Goins' *Wrecked*. Jeff built up a platform quickly by offering advice to writers and by doing lots of guest posting, then he launched a little ebook called "You ARE a writer." The ebook offered positive inspiration for writers and quickly built up his email list.

Then Jeff sent his followers to a book launch page for *Wrecked* full of offers and benefits for people who bought the book, with extras for people who reviewed it. (When Tim Ferriss did this, he threw in some amazing extras like a private dinner cruise with him, for people who bought in bulk).

For example, I could offer something with $100 value for anybody who orders 20 books (this doesn't really work with ebooks—but if the book is available for print, the buyer can give them as gifts or try to resell them). I might not make much profit but my Amazon ranking and media buzz will jump.

I want to sell *as many books as I can as quickly as possible,* even if I'm giving away the profit as rewards. Once my book gets on the bestseller lists, it will probably stay there, because that's the first thing people see on Amazon.

If you plan on advertising, I would do it short-term to correspond with your book launch. An advert in a mass email list or on a website promoting books such as Bookbub.com or Kindle Nation Daily can reach hundreds of thousands of potential readers, but they cost a lot and are usually just for one day. Get that sales rank up as high as you can.

Crowd-source your book launch party

If you're very small and don't have a much of a platform yet, consider teaming up with some other first-time authors. Instead of trying to have a party or event around your book, and having 3 of your friends show up, try to find 10 other local authors and invite them to a "local author book event." If they each bring 3 friends you'll have 30, and it will be much easier to attract media or a newspaper article.

Recently I met the Northwest Independent Writers Association members and authors (niwawriters.com) because they had joined together to fill up a booth of their books at a local festival. Can you make an association like that for your area?

Amazon Associates

If you do have a website, or even if you plan on guest posting or advertising (we will talk about those soon), you should sign up for an Amazon Associates Account. That will allow you to get a special affiliate link to any product on Amazon—so when people visit your website and then click to go buy your book, you'll be making an extra percent of profit from each sale.

But even if they decide not to buy your book, and buy something else, you'll still get your cut! The same thing goes with your links on other sites, or your ads. The special link=more money. Why leave it on the table?

Pinterest and using pictures

Pinterest is a relatively new form of social media; it's mostly like Facebook or Twitter but focuses on sharing pictures. The way many people have been using it for marketing is by turning nice quotes into images. Taking key passages from your writing or blog—a powerful sentence or two at most—and setting it on top of a simple background with a stylish font is an easy way to get you more visibility. If you don't have a background in design, I'd pay for these... spend $50 or $100 to get 10 made (I've used "Ariangga" from fivver.com to do excellent typographic posters).

It's also easy to "double-down" on the material you're already using to gain visitors. For example, you could make a blog post called "100 excellent quotes from books I like" and give brief quotes from 100 favorite books, with a quote from your book somewhere near the top. Then you could make (or hire a designer to make) all of those quotes into a simple picture or image. People who agree with, recognize or like the quote will share it. Very small at the bottom, you could have your name and website.

These pictures could go up on Pinterest, Facebook, and even Twitter. If you were smart, you'd even turn these 100 quotes into a little ebook and make it available online.

If you post them on Facebook, post them as an image, and add text and a link below, rather than as a regular status update. Try to find other things you can post as well... pictures that remind you of your main characters, settings for scene inspiration, book covers you like, great author offices, beautiful natural landscapes for creative inspiration... John Kremer and Joanna Penn are both excellent examples of how to use Pinterest and post a lot of content.

You can even search for stock photography to use with your blog posts and use the same images when you share on social media; images will make everything you do more effective and get more interaction.

Getting into bookstores (indie or otherwise)

In my opinion, focusing your efforts on getting into bookstores is a huge waste of effort and resources.

Anecdote: once I brought my books into Powell's, the major 2nd hand bookstore in Portland Oregon, planning to donate them so that they would be in the shelves and people would see them. The clerk looked up my book in the system and found they already had several copies, and actually they resold pretty quickly. Based on the numbers, he suggested I contact the acquisitions manager to see if they wanted to stock the new book. I did, and despite my efforts, was told that the bookstore doesn't buy self-published books.

The reason is that bookstores like to make direct orders at huge discounts (60% is standard) and don't want to have to pay out thousands of royalty checks to individual authors. You can make your book available, through Lightning Source, at such a discount, but unless your book is already a bestseller or getting lots of media, nobody will order it. Incidentally—I don't recommend Lightning Source: too much work, costly set-up fees, not enough benefits over Createspace.

And yet—if it's already getting tons of media and hitting the bestselling lists, publishers will be coming to you asking you to let them publish it and put it in bookstores! So don't try so hard to get it in bookstores, instead try to build reviews, fanbase, and media coverage, and push up sales.

Something else that should be mentioned: indie authors and indie bookstores appear to be aligned, but this is an illusion. Indie bookstores are trying to make money and stay in business. Amazon is their chief nemesis, and they can't usually take risks on authors. Although some will do you a favor and put your book in their store on consignment, this isn't a very effective form of marketing.

I had a consignment deal set up with about a dozen bookstores: I would send them a couple books, they'd sell them and send me a check for $12 or so, and then I'd send them some more. I soon realized that this wasn't helping me much for the time and effort it took. (I even mailed a box to an indie bookseller in Australia. After shipping costs, I barely broke even.)

If you want to see your name on the shelf, walk into a bookstore, put your book somewhere visible, like right next to bestsellers in your genre, and take a few photos of it there—you can use the photos on your blog or website.

Instead of doing a book signing (which won't spark a lot of interest if you're unknown) organize an "event" around a theme related to yourself or your book. Could you teach a class on self-publishing at the local library? Could you teach a fiction-writing seminar? (Although, if you could, doing so online will be easier and more productive than doing one locally).

Always be thinking about what you're offering people, and how you're benefitting them.

International book fairs

Book fairs are fun events, I've been to most of the big ones around the world. You can pay a fee for a book seller to show off your book in their booth. If you have an interesting enough cover and back copy, you might make a few people interested, and generate a handful of sales. If you're really lucky, you'll get an international publishing scout who will offer foreign translation rights.

The one time I did this, I had several people ask my representative about the book rights and expressing "extreme interest" in re-publishing the book. But, as they realized I was self-published, even though the book was professionally done, the deal fell apart. I believe it's because people in the book industry want to work with agents, and not directly with authors (who can be unprofessional).

Nobody wants to be the first to support a book. If I had already had an agent or US publisher, foreign rights sales would have been pretty easy.

Emailing international publishers about foreign rights failed for similar reasons. Despite all of this, I did sell the foreign rights on my own to a major Russian publisher, but they contacted me directly after seeing my website as a result of my book's media coverage. It was a confusing process, but they finally bank transferred me $1600 for a 4,000 copy first printing of the book, which I consider an achievement.

Focus on Media Coverage and Sales, not bookstores and publishers.

Book award contests

Book award contests are a huge money maker, but not for you. Associations that run book contest charge thousands of authors to enter, and then payout about half the income in awards. I've entered many, and I win about half the time. It's fun to get a plaque or gold sticker or cash bonus and recoup your entrance fee. It can get you a decent amount of exposure and some sales.

And you can write "AWARD-WINNING AUTHOR" or "MULTIPLE AWARD WINNING BOOK" on the top of your cover. You might impress some readers enough to buy. But then, you may also raise expectations and make them more critical than they would otherwise be. I'm not strictly for or against book award contests, but I think you could refrain from entering and not lose out on a lot of sales.

If you do enter and win, as a book cover designer, I should warn you that those "WINNER" award seals can spoil a good cover design. If there's room for it somewhere, fine, but usually it's distracting and mutes the purpose of the cover (which is to create an emotional reaction).

Three things most authors get wrong

If you skipped through this book looking for easy things you can do to boost your book sales, but aren't ready to do anything major, I want to stress again the three critical things that you really need to re-evaluate.

Your book cover is critical to your success. Indie covers are getting better as more high quality graphic designers are focusing on helping out self-publishing authors, but at least half are still bad. *Assume* that your cover isn't good enough, and get some real feedback, ideally from target readers. Most people are too polite to talk about your ugly cover in front of you, so find a way to spy.

Your author website is probably half done, poorly executed and has too little content. About 80% of indie author websites I've looked at have been ugly or unprofessional. If your books are good enough and you have enough reviews, it won't matter—but why make it harder on yourself? It doesn't have to be shiny and glossy. It should be approachable, friendly and honest. Get some feedback and hire a coder or designer at the very least to clean it up and make a nice, professional header.

You start marketing before you have reviews. Indie authors, especially after recent review scandals, are over-sensitive about soliciting reviews and fearful of paying for them. So they start marketing their book with zero reviews. They market hard, and all their efforts are wasted, because nobody wants to be the first person to read and review a book. You need to find a way to get reviews up on Amazon before you seriously promote your book, pay for ads, or do anything else. Don't cheat or pay for fake ones, but strenuously encourage honest reviews and feedback.

Dealing with discouragement

Putting out a book is a huge effort, and it's a profoundly personal experience. It's easy to take every rejection personally. But know that just by finishing your book you've accomplished something few people ever will. And console yourself that most great books weren't appreciated in their time.

If you're sure your book is brilliant, and money isn't the primary issue, I hope you feel proud of yourself for putting it out into the world.

If you plan on writing books as a career choice however, then the money matters.

Don't get discouraged if your first book isn't a smash hit (unless you're writing a non-fiction book meant to support or promote your main business—if this is the case, you can just keep promoting it). Frankly speaking, your first book may not be that good. Most professional and indie authors have several failed books in front of them before they learn the ropes and start making books that sell.

If this is your first book, you've probably written the book you wanted to write without thinking about who would read it. In other words, unlike virtually *all successful businesses*, which start with consumer desire and try to meet a need, you developed the product first assuming people would like it. This means that the odds are most likely against you. Most successful indie authors are writing books in popular genres—and often *they are choosing to do so*.

If you want to become a career author and focus on making obscene amounts of money, before you start writing your next book, consider which genres sell best. Read a few best-selling books in those genres, and think of a similar story, but filtered through your personal experience and writing voice.

The truth is that the vast majority of best-selling books share many similarities, especially fiction. I could write a plot summary for YA paranormal romance or dystopian fiction that would fit 90% of the genre. Don't reinvent the wheel. Identify the patterns, and use them to mold your own story. Is it ART? Is it your soul's passion? Maybe not— but it is vastly more likely to sell books.

You may feel like writing with readers in mind is a pollution of the purity of your creative mind, but if you choose to write for pleasure, don't expect readers to throw money at you. If you want to write novels for money, learn the skills you need, and craft accordingly.

CONCLUSION

There are lots of more specific publicity and marketing tricks you can try. But instead of trying to figure out 1,000 different ways to market your book, you need to focus on what really works, and I've tried to outline that as much as possible. I've also emphasized how important it is to have everything ready before you even think about marketing (I don't know how many times authors have reached out to me, hoping I'll take a look at their book on Amazon, and they don't have any reviews yet, or I catch typos in their book summary). Make sure everything looks amazing, that there is nothing wrong with the sales page, or any other obvious reason you are losing sales. After that, if you're selling a little bit and getting genuine positive reviews, you're ready to start marketing.

It doesn't have to cost any money. If you can't afford a nice cover, do the best you can until your sales give you the funds to upgrade, or check out my DIYbookcovers option.

If you can't afford an editor, force your friends and family to edit your book (editing is non-negotiable. Too many typos will sink any book). Focus on the basics.

If you want quick feedback about your website, sales page or book cover, you can send me an email and I'll try to take a look at it (I probably won't have time to help fix it, but I can identify red flags).

derekmurphy@creativindie.com

SPECIAL UPDATE

I wrote this book at the end of 2013. I stand by my tips on blogging, but the problem with most author websites is A) they're not attractive and professional and B) they are too new, with not enough content to rank well on Google. For this kind of book marketing to be effective, authors need sites where they can guest post and their writings will rank well in search results so people actually find them.

Therefore, I've been buying up high PR, established sites and turning them into large community sites that will benefit lots of authors by encouraging guest posts. These sites are set up to be social, to encourage interaction, comments and guest posting, so that all indie authors can participate and enjoy the benefits. One is for posting book reviews of indie books (reviewing other books in your genre is an excellent way to attract the right kind of readers). Another is for indie publishing news. These are curated, high quality sites — not just content dumps for SEO building. If you'd like to check them out and apply as a guest blogger, send me an email.

Besides book marketing, the other constant challenge for authors is getting book reviews. Check out www.BLURBTRADE.com, a place authors can meet and review each other's books.

CREATIVINDIE

On my blog "Creativindie" I help authors and artists produce and sell their best work, and become financially and creatively independent. One of the fun things I've been doing recently is giving away my TimeShare weeks for authors to use as a "Writer's Vacation." I give away a couple a year, so you may want to join my email list or my Facebook page to stay in the loop.

Feel free to contact me with publishing questions. Although I'm also experimenting with writing and publishing, I've had a lot of experience and am starting to see some huge gains. I hope that together, we can all become fabulously wealthy self-published authors and buy retirement houses in exotic settings, and meet up for martinis and foot massages.

WIN A ONE WEEK RESORT WRITER'S VACATION TO RENEW YOUR CREATIVITY!

If you liked this book, please be generous and give me the gift of a review. It doesn't have to be glowing, only genuine and fair.

ABOUT THE AUTHOR

 DEREK MURPHY has been a book cover designer, writing coach and publishing consultant for almost a decade, working behind the scenes with hundreds of indie and self-publishing authors to make their books more successful. He currently teaches authors and artists how to turn their passions into full-time businesses, make a bigger impact, and blaze a luminous trail of creative independence.

Besides publishing, Derek is an avid traveller with an interest in history and literature. He's lived in Argentina, Malta and Taiwan, and traveled extensively through dozens of countries. He's been a national representative for Amnesty International, and is close to finishing a PHD in Philosophy and Comparative Literature.

Connect with Derek or Twitter or Facebook
Twitter: @creativindie
Facebook: @creativindie
Email: derekmurphy@creativindie.com

CPSIA information can be obtained at www.ICGtesting.com
Printed in the USA
LVOW12s1720050814

397637LV00004B/776/P